WINNING MINDSET

PSYCHOLOGICAL STRATEGIES
THAT **DRIVE** YOU TO **SUCCEED**

DAVID FAIRWEATHER

YOU CAN DOWNLOAD THE **FREE** AUDIOBOOK
VERSION AT **WINNING**-MINDSET.COM

CONTENTS

AKA

WHAT I'VE CALLED THE CHAPTERS AND WHAT ORDER THEY FOLLOW

FOREWORD

AKA

WHO APPROVES OF THIS BOOK?

Anthony T. Galie has been recognized as one of America's hottest speakers. He was selected to speak for the prestigious Million Dollar Round Table (MDRT) – an honour given to less than 1% of all speakers – on four separate occasions, and that's a big deal!

He is an executive coach and author of the business book: *Take Control of Your Subconscious Mind – A Practical Approach to Creating Focus and Becoming More Successful.*

He is most noted for his incredible keynote talk: **The Subconscious Aspects of Business**, which has been presented to over a thousand organizations worldwide. Most notable about his presentation was Anthony's message that high-performers hypnotize themselves, followed by a live demonstration of the phenomenon in action!

Anthony: "May you live in interesting times" is purported to be an ancient Chinese proverb. Some believe that saying the phrase to another is considered a blessing. The sentiment is the hope that you live in a time filled with much opportnity and find many ways to prosper and grow. However, paradoxically for many people, the same phrase is used as a curse. The expression is often used ironically, with the clear implication that 'uninteresting times' of peace and tranquility are more life-enhancing than interesting ones, which from an historical perspective, usually include disorder and conflict.

Few would deny that we are currently living in interesting times. Change is occurring to more people in more areas and industries than in any other time in history. History is rife with seminal moments where, in relatively short periods of time, everything seems to change at once. The old order is rapidly replaced with a new, often entirely different set of norms. Sometimes this happens because a series of events converge, but more often than not, the catalyst is a single event or discovery.

The invention of the plough in 3,000 B.C. meant that we no longer had to keep moving to find food. This almost immediately led to the emergence of the first large civilizations. In 1450, wide use of the printing press allowed dissemination of information to the masses, not just the nobility or the highly educated. The Renaissance soon followed. The steam engine, then the internal combustion engine, rapidly resulting in the modern industrial world we currently live in. History has taught us that **the only thing constant is change**. The changes brought about by such events can affect nearly everyone, but often in very different ways. Those who have vision, foresight, and the strategies to adapt to dramatic change and new realities are far more likely to thrive and prosper, while those who fear change, cling to the past and remain rigid and unyielding, often suffer negative outcomes. They have been referred to those who "are relegated to the dust bin of history."

We are in the midst of the greatest period of change in human history, which is largely the result of a simple alteration in how we count: the conversion from analog to digital. That single change in how we calculate has brought about enormous socio-economic changes to nearly every level of society. The immediate effect was to vastly increase the speed with which we can compute and manipulate data. From that development flowed all manner of changes, inventions, and innovations that have altered nearly every aspect of our lives. It would be impossible to list all the ways the IT revolution has changed and continues to change our lives, but the most obvious game changer for us (other than the internet), is the very recent invention of **the Smartphone**.

And like the aforementioned proverb, some individuals view these interesting times as being filled with opportunity and countless ways to prosper. They embrace change as the vehicle that will take them to a better and brighter place, a chance to learn and experience new things that were inconceivable just a generation ago. They live in a world filled with novel and exciting endless ways to move forward and succeed. Many of these individuals actually describe their journey to success and prosperity as being "fun". That attitude is simply a by-product of their mindset.

Others perceive these changing times as a threat. Their habitual behaviour is driven by a fear of losing what they have, not on *getting something better*. These individuals have difficulty seeing where they would fit in this new world and dread the thought of having to change their habits. Just as the proverb illustrates, "interesting" can be either a curse or a blessing. The question becomes: why is it one way for some, and the opposite for others?

Events perceived as positive or negative are predicated on an individual's state of mind, or "mindset." In fact, our experiences are more heavily influenced by our state of mind and perception than by our actual reality. A positive, or winning mindset can often mean the difference between success or failure in any endeavour.

Most people are unaware of the power and effects of their mindset. Thus, they often feel out of control of their behaviour and environment and believe that much of what happens to them is "luck" or "fate". Essentially, they are pawns in the game of life who feel helpless and largely unable to control their own destiny. There is a famous aphorism attributed (incorrectly) to Thoreau. It reads: "**Most men lead lives of quiet desperation and die with their song still inside them.**" Even though Thoreau didn't write it, that phrase does beautifully capture what many people, who do not know how to direct and control their mindset, spend much of their lives feeling.

However, some high-performing individuals not only recognize the power of their mindset but have learned to control it. Somewhere in their life they were either taught how to control it, or by trial and error, mastered techniques that allow them to tap into their subconscious mind to utilize its benefits whenever needed. There is also a group who know about the effects of their mindset, and how beneficial it can be when used properly, but simply do not know how to tap into it or where they can learn how.

David Fairweather noticed the effects and benefits of a winning mindset early on in his career and has spent years studying the phenomenon. Through careful research he has compiled many different ways to produce powerful shifts in people's state of mind. Recognizing that different personality types tend to respond to different approaches, David has developed a variety of simple but powerful methods systematically designed to produce positive results. Results that work for nearly anyone who is open to following a few easy-to-understand directions, and willing to spend a little time practicing his methods.

David's research has shown that there are many practical applications for a motivated mindset. Willing participants often reported ancillary benefits such as an increase in feelings of wellbeing, reduced levels of stress, increased confidence, and other positive mental effects. In addition, job performance, accuracy, positive attitude, and other measures of physical acuity often increased as well.

David's book, *Winning Mindset*, is the best compilation of techniques and practical applications on the subject that I have ever read. I unhesitatingly recommend it to anyone interested in learning how to use the power of their mind to improve themselves in their business, as well as their personal lives. I fully expect this book to change many lives for the better and I commend David on a job very well done.

If standing out in your field or getting ahead of the curve is something you want for yourself, you are only a few pages away from discovering the psychological strategies used instinctively by high-performers and visionary thinkers. Congratulations on getting this book. I know you are in for a treat.

Wishing you all the 'luck' your purposeful application of the techniques within these pages will afford you. May you truly live in and prosper from, incredibly interesting times. Like David says, *You Can Do It!*

Anthony T. Galie

June 1, 2018

DAVID FAIRWEATHER

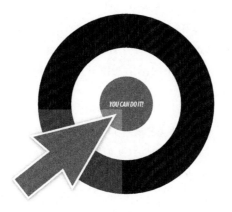

INTRODUCTION

WHAT YOU WILL LEARN

AKA

WHY READ THIS BOOK

Given the choice, wouldn't you want to:

- **Be** more focused?

- **Feel** more motivated?

- **Perform** at a higher level?

Well, you do have a choice. I'm going to show you how to:

MAKE THE CHOICE AND MAKE IT HAPPEN

This isn't just a book focused on mindset: It's also a book about getting and staying motivated. This is a book about staying focused. In reality, this is a book about employing your subconscious mind to take care of things, so that it becomes almost effortless for you. Most people don't realize how much they lose sight of what they aren't focused on and how it can affect them. I share throughout this book how to stay focused and accomplish more.

The concepts and strategies that we'll explore together can be used in pretty much any area of your life that you'd like to improve. We are going to focus primarily on aspects that can be considered competitive, where standing out from the pack would be advantageous for you, like in your career, but we'll also touch on some health and wellness tips too since these strategies work on any goal you could set for yourself. The tips and tricks you are going to learn will give you an edge over the average employee, entrepreneur or business owner, but only if you put them to use!

Success isn't easy, and that's a good thing – at least in business. If it was easy, everybody would be doing it and your competition would be outrageous! But everybody isn't doing it. This is a book about why they aren't doing it and why you can do it. You've already taken a step further than the average wishful thinker. You've taken action by buying this book, and that's just one of the things that is going to distinguish you from everyone else.

Everyone gets powerfully motivated to make a significant change in their life from time to time. Some examples of goal setting categories are: a **personal** goal to get healthy, run a marathon, slim down, stop smoking or learn a new language. We could set an **interpersonal** goal to improve a relationship, be nicer to restaurant staff, make new friends or to save a marriage. A career-oriented person might decide to set a **business** goal to get promoted, earn a bigger bonus, win an award, or dominate a new niche or territory. You could consider a **financial** goal to fatten up your retirement fund and optimize investments to secure your future. A **community** goal to get more involved in a social group, help out a good cause or charitable organization can have a lasting effect far beyond your immediate circle. We can all set goals for ourselves, but most people find it hard to remain motivated long enough to successfully implement the new habit in their life, and tend to effortlessly fall back into their old, familiar, but ineffective habits.

This is a book about the habits of highly successful people. High achievers and top performers certainly aren't average, but they definitely aren't superhuman—even if you currently see them that way. You might have even told yourself that you could never be one of them. Well, they are human beings just like you and me. They experience regular problems, just like we do. But somehow, they don't allow life to get in the way of their dreams and aspirations.

This book explains some of the fundamental psychological principles they use in setting themselves up to succeed in whatever they set their mind to. Many of them so habitually that they might not even be consciously aware that they are doing it. There are no difficult methods between these pages, only hands on techniques that you can easily implement as soon as you've read them. When you change the way you think about what's possible for you to achieve, you can begin the process of bettering your life in whatever way you'd love to change.

You are going to learn that your biggest problem is *you*. And that's a good thing. If you really are the problem, you can learn to stop subconsciously sabotaging your success, and start making the kind of progress that becomes almost effortless. Yes, the masters of any industry or any endeavour make it look easy – and for them it is. But it rarely starts out that way for anyone.

We've all got our challenges in life, but if you believe you have what it takes to rise to the challenge you face, you definitely have what it takes to succeed despite the odds. Self-belief is a powerful thing that money just cannot buy. I can't give it to you and you can't find it in a seminar. What I can give you is a deep understanding of where it comes from and how to go about making more of it.

YOUR BIGGEST INFLUENCER

Simply put: how you see yourself, and what you say to yourself, reinforces your expectations and sets you up for your experiences. It sounds simple because it is simple. I'm not going to make it complicated, but I am going to invest a little time to help you get clear on what's really possible for you if you really want to know.

I'm going to show you that what you *feel* determines what you *do*, and what you *do* determines how you *feel*. I'm going to change the way you might think and teach you how to gain more control over your results. It's my goal to help you banish self-doubt, and to get over your inner critic that holds you back.

I'm going to teach you why that annoying voice exists within you in the first place, and I'm going to give you the tools you need to go way beyond wishful thinking and make your dreams a reality. This is the time to stop making excuses and get with the program of performing at a higher level. You are not defined by your past, you are defined by your actions today.

Ready to go from being someone who occasionally tries and too often gives up, to someone that doesn't let anything get in the way of achieving their goals?

If your answer is "no", then sit back and accept life the way it is without any expectation of achieving anything more. I'd prefer you didn't lower the success rates of my readership by telling yourself not to bother trying or insisting that it's impossible to change. You get what you make of life, and so I need you to give me a "hell, yeah!".

If the word "hell" offends you and provocative words freak you out, I highly recommend finding a nice old lady or a sweet old man in a beige cardigan to comfortably coach you. If, on the other hand, you are looking to get provoked and propelled into action, I think you are going to like the journey you've already begun with me.

I may know a lot about human nature and personality types, but if I don't know you personally, I obviously won't yet know exactly what you need to know and how you'll interpret these words. So, bear with me for a bit.

All I ask is that you read it with an open mind and that you don't jump to any conclusions prematurely. Giving up too quickly might just be the problem. I promise I won't use many long words and you have my word that every concept in this book has some science to back it up.

This isn't questionable advice from some self-appointed expert. This is sage advice from someone that has done more than his fair share of skepticism. I didn't start off this annoyingly positive. I've invested tens of thousands of dollars into training with some of the most motivational mentors on the planet. Now these days, I'm a true believer in what's possible for someone determined to overcome the "curse of average". Maybe it's not as bad as hell, but to my mind, average is a far worse curse.

We are going to take this in simple steps. Please don't jump around and cherry-pick chapters. That's just a clever way to fail at improving. I can't help you if you are going to insist on doing it your way. If you already know what to do, I wonder, "why you are reading this?" I'm not suggesting that you won't already know some of this, or that any of it isn't kind of obvious at some level.

What I am suggesting is that by reading this book from cover to cover, page by page, <u>in order</u>, you might just get better at being the best you that you can be. It's really not a big book, but you could really find it useful to read it through once or twice, or even thrice if you like it as much as I expect you will.

I wish someone would have taken the time to get through to me how much our habitual thoughts affect us when I was burning out as a hired gun in the high-tech world of automotive design. My doctor told me I'd have carpal tunnel syndrome and an over-excited nervous system for the rest of my life. It wasn't the brightest outlook, to be sentenced to a life of pain. But a determined mind, armed with some simple neuroscience, and a creative imagination, can cause a lot of surprising changes to take place.

I learnt the hard way how negative self-talk, a poor perspective, and expecting the worse can have a powerful influence, that make what you really want, almost impossible to achieve. The solution is simple.. Knowing how to change it isn't enough by itself though, you have to apply some of the techniques. Together we are going to look at a lot of practical ways that you can influence yourself to change for the better.

The first step – is don't let someone convince you that you are condemned to suffer a life of frustration and disappointment. Your future hasn't happened yet, and you don't know what you can accomplish until you try. Really try. **In life and in business, you can adopt the mindset of a winner or the mindset of a loser – you decide.**

Are you sitting uncomfortably? Great, then let's begin...

DAVID FAIRWEATHER

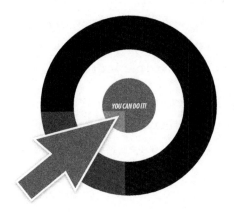

CHAPTER 1

WHAT'S SO HARD ABOUT CHANGE?

AKA

WHY FAILURE IS SO MUCH EASIER TO ACHIEVE

The human mind is capable of amazing things. It guides our thinking and drives our bodies. It thrives on efficiency and achieves it by forming habits that free us up from having to think about things we've already learned. Your first driving lesson was likely quite overwhelming. You probably would not have coped well with the radio on and noisy passengers who insisted on holding a conversation with you, while you were struggling to pay attention to the traffic, all those mirrors, and your new controls and gauges.

After a few lessons and some time spent on the road you probably felt a lot less overwhelmed. Somewhere around your driving test or shortly afterwards, driving became a lot less stressful. Your ability to take on new tasks like changing the radio station and singing along with your favourite song, became a lot less challenging for you. You became more energy efficient.

The act of driving didn't change, but the way your brain processed the skill altered significantly. Instead of having to consciously focus on every movement to get it right, the muscle memories became conditioned in your body and driving progressed from active working memory to passive long-term memory in your brain. Driving became something you no longer needed to pay attention to consciously, and you were able to trust your deeper unconscious mind and body to do it for you.

The same thing happens to me every January: if I don't pay attention, I end up writing the wrong year on the top of my first few client note pages. By mid-January, writing the correct year has again become a learned habit and I can mindlessly note the right year for another eleven months. Changing from January to February brings its own challenge, but thanks to my smartphone, I get a visual reminder about which month it is every day. Of course, if I don't notice, I can write the wrong month at first, and sometimes more than once!

Our capacity for automaticity that allows us to think about other things and focus elsewhere when performing routine tasks can keep us stuck in familiar habits and make changing hard to do. Habits become comfortable and familiar, and brains stuck in learned habits can be very resistant to changing.

Once something has become a habit to us, we rarely need to pay attention when doing it. In fact, once we have become habituated to something, we often don't even notice it. Have you noticed that the word cult is hidden in the word culture? It's in plain sight, but people are often surprised to see it when I point it out to them. I had a habit of thinking of myself as a CAD Expert (aka 3D Design Guru), and I couldn't see myself doing anything else – until I was forced to go back to school, and change how I earned my living at the turn of the 21st century.

One of the university projects I assisted on back in my research days, was focused on the Canadian enculturation of nurses educated elsewhere on the planet. What they hadn't been exposed to previously, and what the university had not previously seen as necessary to teach them, was making it hard for them to fit in. Some of the lessons they needed to learn were "so obvious" that no-one had noticed before. They weren't all life or death lessons like, "what is the correct procedure if a doctor is suspected of making a mistake on a medication order?", but they were all aimed at teaching the nurses how to perform at the highest level of competence possible under pressure.

You might not think you have many life or death moments in your average day, but some habits you've learned literally save your life like:

Looking left and right before crossing the road

Always coming to a complete stop at red lights and stop signs

The list isn't endless, but knowing the rules of the road makes it safer to get where you are headed. Thankfully, the Highway Code thought to provide its readers with lots of examples about what to do if this or that happens on the road. Once you've committed them to your long-term memory, you don't have to hold them in your mind.

It's so easy for something to become such second nature that you no longer think about it. With some things, we can become so deeply habituated into not noticing them consciously, that we are unaware just how much they influence us. The elusive obvious isn't instantly apparent (obviously!). We have the power to discard from consciousness, what is always there, and only notice novel things brought to our attention. Habituation is human nature. People really are creatures of habit.

EVERYDAY BLINDNESS

Can you still smell the cologne, deodorant or perfume you put on this morning? Don't use scents? What about the smell of your laundry detergent or fabric softener on your clothes? I'm willing to bet that you noticed the smell of your house or apartment when you were considering buying or renting it, but have no clue what it smells like today, unless you recently filled it with a novel odour, like "burnt pizza" from an accident in your oven. You probably don't think it smells like anything these days. It's surprisingly easy to become blind to what is always there. If you've seen one of my YouTube videos or we've become friends on Facebook, you probably think I have an accent, but that you don't.

I have an English accent and changing it would take effort. When I first emigrated to Canada I occasionally struggled with people not understanding my style of English. Canadian is different, eh. I had no idea that my Queen's English was difficult to understand until it was repeatedly brought to my attention. If everyone had just smiled at me and nodded, I might not have developed a habit of speaking in a flattened version of my speech patterns to sound clearer to North American ears. Now, I am easily understood, but some people think I have an Australian accent today!

Why am I telling you this, you may wonder? Well, to answer that, let's look at the main causes of failing to try (other than sheer laziness) – getting stuck:

THE THREE WAYS PEOPLE GET AND STAY STUCK

1. **VISUALLY:** They have a habit of not noticing that they are stuck (or seeing that there is a way out).

2. **AUDITORILY:** They have a habit of telling themselves that they are stuck (or hearing others tell them that they are).

3. **KINAESTHETICALLY:** They've been conditioned to feel that they are stuck, and it has become a habit!

Some people daydream about having a bigger house, a newer car or a flatter stomach. They might even tell people about their dreams in a way that sounds like it might happen but do very little about it other than dream. Thinking about what you wish for yourself is called wishful thinking. Daydreaming about a better life that you are not putting in the effort to make real, is merely a dream. Don't get me wrong, it's great to have dreams.

But if you are going to make a significant change to your status quo, doing something about it is a necessary part of the process.

If you ask the average salesperson what their goal for the next five years is, they might know, or they might just shrug. But ask them what their goal for the coming week is, and they'll probably glaze over or look confused. It's one thing having a big goal, but without smaller goals that lead us there, how could we expect to be making the right kind of progress to reach our desired destination? We'd be wandering around almost aimlessly, and an unguided missile isn't likely to hit its target.

Could you imagine desiring to graduate university but not focusing on completing your weekly assignments? Would you really study effectively if you had not sorted through your strengths and weaknesses and assessed what your learning priorities were?

Aimless, unfocused people only get successful by accident. Unguided missiles hit what is in their path and never go out of their way, even when there are far more strategic targets they could have aimed at. They hit what they hit and miss everything else. If you do not study the highway code, its improbable that you will know what to do when you encounter a red light. Some people get frozen when faced with a decision, and it's very often useful to know what you will do in the eventuality that you encounter a green light.

GETTING LUCKY

Occasionally, a sales agent thinking on their feet, comes up with the perfect thing to say to a prospective customer. But the odds of that aren't something to bet on. Everyone can flub their way awkwardly though a chance meeting with a highly desirable client, but if you are not prepared for that chance elevator meeting, you are not likely to hit the ground floor running. When you are trying to sell yourself on a diet in the middle of a banquet or buffet, the same need exists.

Maybe I'm opening your eyes to the fact that a lack of preparation prevents you from having an impact, but even if I do get you motivated, chances are it won't last for very long. We've all heard countless stories from friends and relatives about how "this year is going to be different". New gym memberships overload gym owners every January, but by February, many of the new year members are no longer making it in to work out. Motivation is a fleeting thing that requires nurturing for it to grow into a fully-fledged habit.

Smokers routinely decide that tomorrow they will stop smoking, only to change their mind the next evening, if not the next morning! It seems we cannot really expect motivation to last any longer than 48 hours, and, maybe a lot less. Waning motivation is a significant problem, and stems from a misunderstanding about where it comes from and how to make more of it.

High performers and top achievers have got this figured out... or they would all merely be exceptional flukes. They develop habits that we'd be lucky to have. Outliers and exceptions are everywhere, but we shouldn't base our goals on getting lucky. The more strategically you hone in on the right next step for you to take, the luckier you'll get. A successful parachute jump is statistically more likely with a well-packed parachute, than simply crossing your fingers and hoping it deploys.

Statistically, there are far more people who feel uncomfortable about doing things differently, than there are people who are comfortable to make significant changes with any regularity. Why is that, you wonder? Simply put: there is no change without stress. Stress is an adaptation process, and any need to change will necessitate at least some stress. Even *thinking* about change causes many people to feel anxious. Intuitively, we do not want to experience anxiety and we'd generally prefer to suffer as little stress as possible. Stress and anxiety keep us from making progress when we feel compelled to avoid them at all costs.

THERE IS A PRICE TO PAY FOR EVERYTHING

The cost of avoiding all stress and anxiety would be death. Stress is the price we pay for being alive and some degree of anxiety is the anticipatory fear we feel whenever we enter the unknown. Some people purposefully avoid facing the unknown by convincing themselves that they are where they want to be. Our brains can convince us not to try to change, because change brings with it a threat to what already is.

Q: How do you avoid getting scared by a horror film?

A: Don't watch it.

Q: How do you totally avoid being afraid of change?

A: Don't do it.

There is really nothing to fear when you are making a positive change, but it still imposes a threat to the status quo of your life and the homeostasis of your body as far as your brain is concerned. Many changes present a lot of threats.

It's all well and good leaving a conference pumped up to implement a new sales strategy or deciding that now is the time to get fit, after being motivated by a relatable keynote. The problem is, your brain is not trying to bring uncomfortable changes into being. And unless you are persistent in working to change, what already is will more likely persist.

Changing your mind about needing to change your behaviour, makes it unnecessary for you to have to make progress. With motivation waning rapidly with every hour that passes, the odds of successfully implementing the new way of being, becomes less and less likely the longer you wait to act.

Your brain is made to make decisions and act on them instantly. It assesses circumstances and situations and mobilizes you to act on things you feel strongly about. Give yourself time to think about not doing it, and your feelings are likely to diminish in intensity.

Thinking about moving out of the way of a moving car could just get you run over and living a lifetime of regret (if you survive). We were not engineered to relentlessly ponder action. We were made to act now. We are moved to act by emotion, but emotions are fleeting and do not last indefinitely.

THE GOOD, THE BAD, AND THE UNDECIDED

"Analysis paralysis" is an overwhelming and immobilizing, cognitive conflict brought about by entertaining too many choices. We are complex beings, we humans, but we are also very simple indeed. Our dualistic, binary brains process everything as either good or bad. Things don't start off inherently either, but our categorizing mind manipulates everything into being one or the other. Jokes are not good or bad, you decide. A four-year-old might have a different opinion, and you get to decide if their opinion is good or bad.

All commercial songs and movies are dependent on public opinion to be considered successful, even though their songwriters and directors might love them passionately, regardless of however they are received and reviewed by the public. People can disagree, because we do not all make the same decisions about everything. Bad is a decision, not an actuality.

Your reality is influenced by what you consider to be good or bad, and if you have decided it is scary rather than exciting to make a change, you'd have to really force yourself to suffer it. Forced changes rarely take long-term, because we really are motivated to feel good overall. We were designed to cope with short-term stress and for some brief time we can suffer with it. But ceaseless stress wears us out eventually. Your body and brain need downtime.

You cannot endure an unending stress response, as you will from time to time need to enjoy some relaxing rest time. An overwhelming goal that is not achieved quickly runs the risk of eventually losing its lure.

Our fight or flight response propels us to attack or retreat instinctively. We'd rather rest and digest, and many of us routinely entertain pleasurable pastimes that provide us with immediate gratification. We are drawn to what feels good, but right now, not forever.

The promise of fun in three years from now is not very tantalizing. Similarly, with pain, we can race away from an attacking tiger, but if the tiger never loses its steam, eventually we will lose our life. A big goal you cannot achieve anytime soon, is a long-term threat to your nervous system that would deter you from persisting with it. Fun in three hours from now, is a more immediate lure that has the power to drive us to completing the task standing in our way.

Unless you really expect to cash in on your efforts and can almost taste the success now, your motivation is bound to diminish. Without a realistic expectation of relief, the tension of trying will tend not to endure for very long at all.

Subconscious expectations influences change far more than conscious desire does. Desire to change with a low expectation of success does not have a good prognosis, or at least I'VE decided that it's bad. You might choose to disagree, but I'd rather you argue with Dr. Donald Price at the University of Florida, who I expect will win the argument based on science. Of course, you won't need to do that, because I'm going to be proving it to you conclusively in a later chapter.

INABILITY TO ADAPT

I know what makes sense to me. I have my way of thinking, and of course that is an habitual thought habit that I'm resistant to changing. I can't make the claim that I'm addicted to my mindset, but I'd like to think that we can agree that I am somewhat addicted to doing things that feel good? I'm certainly not addicted to doing things that feel bad! You could disagree with my use of the word addiction, but if we weren't addicted to our habits to some degree, we wouldn't even stress out a tiny bit when something gets in the way of us doing them. We are all pleasure addicts in some measure, but some of us have greater control over our addictions than others.

Some people lie to themselves incessantly and deceptively. They lie to themselves so well that they are convinced that they are telling the truth. "It can't be done" and "I can't do it" stop us from trying in vain. "I'll make the call tomorrow" and "I'll start my diet tomorrow" are fabulous ways of delaying the sense of failure. The reward for self-deception is feeling a false sense of control right now.

Tomorrow is an elusive concept, since you only experience reality in the now. Yesterday is a fading memory and tomorrow never comes. All you have is this moment, and if you have a problem with self-deception but you aren't yet convinced that you have a problem, it's statistically unlikely that you'll overcome it any time soon. You can't fix what you aren't aware of.

Fear of the unfamiliar along with fear of failure, go hand in hand with any change you are contemplating, at least in some measure. Statistically, pessimists might have a more accurate take on reality, but optimists in general, are predictably happier and live longer lives. Having a positive outlook about your ability to make a change, is going to keep your dream alive longer than giving up because it's "pointless". Odds are, if you are sick of failing, you'll probably give up. But you do not have to. You can defy the odds by doing something different, because, doing what failed before won't change anything.

The bell curve from statistics show us that in any randomized grouping of people there will always be predictable tendencies.

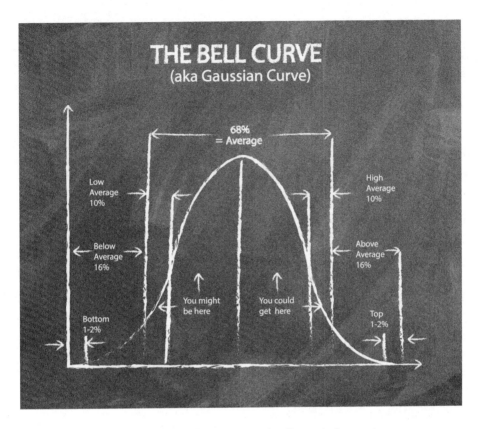

It doesn't just predict quality control of manufacturing processes and the range of intellects within a class of college students. It also points out to us, that in any group of people, like a room full of entrepreneurs, an international sales team, a support group for dieters, or a classroom of psychology students, there will always be those that gravitate towards excellence, those that feel more comfortable being mediocre or average, and a few that always fall predictably below average.

A small percentage of them (around 1 or 2 percent) will perform extremely poorly, and a similar percentage will perform unbelievably well. Performing well or under par, like most human abilities, are part nature and part nurture. Freaks of nature do occur, but not often. Often those that get focused get seen to do better. Nature might inform us, but we are certainly entitled to our own opinion.

If you consider yourself an average performer or an unexceptional human being, you are not as locked into place as you might believe. Of course, it comes at a cost, but you can get a big return on your investment if you are willing to work at change. Average is simply a conditioned state of being. Undeveloped talent can be developed, and unnurtured nature can naturally be nurtured intentionally if the opportunity to improve is noticed and not negated. I'm attempting to communicate that possibility to you right now, but I cannot guarantee that you will agree with me, even if you should.

Don't misunderstand me. I'm not saying that it's likely you can go from amongst the poorest 1 or 2% of the population to being one of the wealthiest people on the planet, or from the world's worst guitar player or pianist, to one of the best on the planet. You might not easily enter the top 1 or 2% of the exceptional if you are a late starter or not naturally inclined towards mega-achievements. But you can certainly make improvements on your current status with a little bit of strategy and a generous serving of optimism.

You can definitely skew the curve in your favour with some well-directed effort. Just because something doesn't come naturally to you, it doesn't mean you can't learn how to do it, make improvements and eventually master it. Even if it seems impossible at first. We learn something from getting our car stuck in a ditch, sliding uncontrollably on ice or getting a flat.

We learn a lot about ourselves when we are forced to confront a breakdown.

You might respond terribly at first, but since we learn from trial and error, your errors are incredibly valuable in the learning process. Giving up quickly secures failure far faster than any enduring or persisting ever could. Being willing to persist despite some bad experiences on the way to mastery, will tell you everything you need to know about your capacity to succeed.

The simple formula for success is this: **if you want to succeed — never give up.** To help you understand what is possible for someone determined to shift a powerful paradigm, let's look at some of world's most successful people and see what we can learn from them, just as soon as we've had a quick look at a few standout learnings from the last few pages:

CHAPTER 1 SUMMARY

AKA:

WHAT YOU'VE LEARNED BY READING THIS CHAPTER

1. Human beings are creatures of habit and habits don't require mental effort. So, make habits that support your goals and achieving them will become much easier.

2. If you believe you are stuck, then you are stuck. But if you believe there is a way out, and you never stop seeking it and you will find it.

3. Targets are a great deal easier to hit on purpose when you have a clear view of them. So be clear and aim well.

4. Stress is an adaptation process that uses your vitality as currency. Spend your life well and don't waste energy habitually.

5. The odds are that you are average, but you can certainly skew the odds by doing what exceptional people do.

DAVID FAIRWEATHER

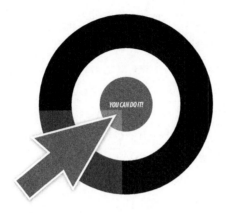

CHAPTER 2

HABITS OF THE HIGHLY SUCCESSFUL

AKA

HOW HIGH PERFORMERS MAKE IT LOOK EASY

I have fun pointing out the "elusive obvious" to the teams that I speak to and the people I coach. One of the most basic and obvious concepts that people like to argue about is the idea of nature or nurture. Nothing is ever exclusively one or the other. Nothing. It is not possible for any one-dimensional truth to exist as a fact that cannot be disputed. There are always two sides to every disagreement and argument. What some think of as wrong or bad, others may think of as right or good. What some see as a problem, others can see as a challenge. Your truth is merely an opinion that you are free to cling to until contrary evidence surfaces, or you decide to change it.

Even the existence of light brings with it at least two sides. Does light happen or is light a thing? There is a fundamental duality paradox between particles and waves, neither being exclusively either, and are only determined at any given time dependent on the context of observation (aka perception). A photon is a light particle and the flow of the photon is a wave. Light is neither matter nor motion, it is both at the same time, depending on your perception. Einstein explained this by saying, "We have two contradictory pictures of reality: separately neither of them fully explains the phenomena of light, but together they do".

There are always at least two sides to everything in a three-dimensional universe, and you can quote me on that. You cannot have up without down, good without bad, or dark without light. Our brains learn by comparison and pattern matching. This looks like that, that is like this. Good is not like bad, and bad is unlike good. If everything in our universe was always "good", we simply wouldn't need the word "good" in our language.

So, it's never nature OR nurture, it's always both to some degree. And that's a good thing—unless you think it's a bad thing? Nature is formed by nurture and nurture is informed by nature. They go hand in hand and are as inseparable as your mind and body.

Numerous psychological studies have been conducted that look at the influence of environment and genetics on pairs of twins. They are called twin studies. Genetically identical twins have been studied where both possess the gene for schizophrenia, but each were adopted by different families into different environments. The results of those studies have clearly shown that being born with a genetic capacity (nature) is only one side of the trait puzzle. It takes a stressful environment (nurture) to trigger the schizophrenia gene into expressing itself. Neither twin is guaranteed to become a schizophrenic. Why am I telling you this? I want you to know that you are not entirely predefined by your genes, even though they do have an influence over your natural abilities and your potential.

Nature doesn't trick us with as many limitations as some people might be inclined to think. We learn most of them. For example, we all were born with the capacity to communicate. We weren't however preprogrammed with any particular language. It would be very weird for a child born in China to Chinese parents, in a Mandarin speaking family, to spontaneously start to speak German without learning it from somewhere! We have the natural capacity to communicate, but we have to learn the language that we encounter in our environment if we want to be understood and to understand others. If we do not learn to communicate effectively enough to get our needs met, that's on us or a deficiency of nurturing from our parents and teachers, but not nature.

In addition to the components of communication, we also get taught what is (and what is not) possible by those that learned before us. It's good to think that a human being cannot fly from the top of a tall building. That protects future generations from harming themselves by naively trying. But the thought, "humans can never fly" is bad if it closes off the possibility of even imagining a solution.

In the beginning of the 20th century, visionary thinker Orville Wright was determined to make a man fly. He firmly believed that somehow it was possible, and he was absolutely determined to figure out how. Apart from being famous for inventing the first power-driven airplane along with his brother Wilbur, Orville Wright is also famous for declaring that: "If we all worked on the assumption that what is accepted as true is really true, there would be little hope of advance". It was not that the Wright Brothers were better educated than everyone else and knew better. In fact, neither of them finished high school and could both be considered dropouts. What they *did* have was a vision of the future.

It seems true visionaries do not lock themselves into the same views as the average person. Without rule breakers and chance takers, progressing out of the ordinary is not an inevitability.

Another visionary rule breaker who has changed how human beings think about what is possible is Sir Roger Bannister. Bannister is famous for being the first man in history to break the four-minute mile. He was told that it was impossible for a human being to do, but Roger did not want to believe that attempting to do it would be futile. He was determined to prove that it was possible, and in 1954, he did exactly that. He didn't even train that hard, but he held onto a certainty that it was possible. He told others that it could be done and that he was going to do it. More importantly, he told himself that he could do it and that he *was going to do it*.

The accepted human speed limit for running a mile until then had been capped at 15 MPH. The cultural belief was that running faster than that for a full mile was absolutely impossible. He may only have broken the record by 0.6 of a second in 1954, but he also broke something that was much bigger: the limiting belief that was held by everyone else. The influence of his belief lead yet another runner to break Bannister's new record less than seven weeks later! Since then, over the last 50 years, 17 additional seconds have been shaved off the old four-minute mile myth and many other people have also accomplished the once-impossible feat.

YOU ARE NOT BOUND TO FAIL

Being bound by the reality of the average person will limit anyone to staying unexceptional. Let's face it, by definition most people are average, and exceptional people stand out from them as in some way special. They don't often possess anything that the average person doesn't have, they just refuse to accept the idea that what they want to accomplish is not possible. There are always standouts in every sales team that defy the expectations of their competition. Those of us that don't let go of their dream of doing something incredible with the time that life affords them, will accomplish a great deal more than the average person is expected to achieve.

Another incredible visionary that has defied being ordinary is Oprah Winfrey. She did not come from a wealthy family and definitely did not have the support of her abusive father. But, according to Forbes Real Time Net Worth, Oprah Winfrey has earned a net worth of almost three billion dollars to date. That's quite a feat for a woman of colour to achieve in a country that not very long ago would not have allowed her onto the same bus as a white woman. Back when Sir Roger was breaking the laws of running, Oprah's family would have been punished for attempting to quench their thirst at a public drinking fountain.

Oprah might not be famous for being the first African-American billionaire, but she is famous for being the first female African-American billionaire. How did she do it? By not listening to naysayers and by not believing her original agent when he told her that she could not demand more than $250,000 a year for her talk show. Everyone told her that he was right, but Oprah chose not to buy into that limiting belief. Today, she is one of Forbes' 400 richest people on the planet and has been quoted as saying: "I don't have any limitations on what I think I could do or be". Now she makes almost a million dollars a day and over $25,000,000 a month!

Oprah has developed unwavering self-belief and is not bound by the same limiting beliefs about what is possible that keeps success beyond the reach of the average business woman, black, white or otherwise. She is a proponent of mindfulness, meditation and self-hypnosis as methods of mastering your mind and overcoming the curse of average. She can be seen online sitting with Deepak Chopra exploring the power of her mind in 1993 with a simple experiment that we will be doing together in a later chapter. If you seek out the video to watch, you'll see clearly that the ideas held in our mind influence us outside of awareness.

In 2014, Forbes Magazine published an article claiming that many of the world's most successful business leaders have been hypnotizing themselves to do better in business. The list of visionaries that envision themselves breaking down barriers and unburdening themselves from self-limiting beliefs is extraordinary. From Wolfgang Amadeus Mozart, Thomas Edison and Winston Churchill, to Ellen DeGeneres, Tony Robbins and David Beckham, you'll find evidence online that many of today's top athletes, coaches, celebrities, politicians, CEO's and entrepreneurs, all share something in common. They have all tapped into the power of their own mind to develop an unwavering belief in what is truly possible for them.

TAPPING INTO EXCELLENCE

Sylvester Stallone, Matt Damon and Kevin Costner have all utilized the services of a hypnotist during their careers and are happy to rave about their experience. Jessica Alba and Kate Middleton have both given birth without painkillers by employing a hypnotist to help them overcome the tension-building fear, that causes pain and plagues most mothers-to-be on the planet. Julia Roberts and Bruce Willis have both employed a hypnotist to overcome a debilitating stutter. (Are you surprised to learn that they ever stuttered?) World class golfers Jack Nicklaus and Tiger Woods have both benefitted immensely from working with a hypnotist to develop greater focus, block out distractions and to visualize success on the green. Clearly, it worked for them!

Not limited to golfers and actors, anyone interested in the success habits of high-performers will find article after article online about the self-affirming beliefs cultivated in the minds of the world's highest achievers by professionals like myself who are hired to affect the kinds of paradigm shifts that the late, great Stephen Covey strongly suggested we need. Companies like IBM, Ford, KFC, Pepsi, Re/Max, DuPont, Federal Express, Panasonic, Bell and Bombardier have not only all employed hypnotists to entertain their staff at parties, but it seems that they are all at the forefront of a growing trend. Multimillion dollar corporations are bringing in hypnotic heavyweights to help train the minds of their go-getters to do better and go further in their field than the average employee.

Every company has a culture and the cultural landscape is shifting rapidly in the direction of mind-focused methods for achieving excellence. Call it mindfulness, purposeful mindfulness, visualization, sensualization or self-hypnosis, people are using it to get hyper-focused and mega successful! They've been using it since the dawn of time, but it doesn't need to be shrouded in mysticism. It can easily be used with a little guidance from someone you trust.

As I've mentioned, unless what you want to achieve is actually impossible (whatever that means), the only thing holding you back from achieving it is you. Every great athlete has a great coach that encourages them. Every great actor has a great acting coach and an exceptional director directing them. Great executives have great executive coaches and high reaching entrepreneurs employ specialists in every aspect of their business to circumvent the time it takes to learn by trial and error alone.

The science of human performance is not exactly complicated, but it does require utilizing if you aren't determined to stumble upon its principles yourself. We can definitely learn from others if we are open to what their lessons can teach us. What are some of the habits of high achievers in your industry or area of interest? It's one thing to fall prey to a compelling marketing campaign offering shortcuts and quick hacks, but following an evidence-based protocol that has worked for many others is going to give you far greater certainty of succeeding.

ARE YOU QUALIFIED TO SUCCEED?

It might defy a cultural belief, but academic credentials are not a necessary component of being a top performer. Sure, good knowledge is great to "learn", especially if you are going to be a doctor, lawyer or engineer, but there have been many other high school and college dropouts like the Wright brothers that have achieved incredible accolades in their field. The two most obvious examples are Bill Gates and Steve Jobs. Neither of them finished college because they both shared a vision of dominating the personal computer industry with competing companies Microsoft and Apple. Mark Zuckerberg, the mind behind a little thing called Facebook, dropped out of Harvard. And media mogul Russell Simmons dropped out of Manhattan College just prior to finishing his sociology degree.

Ellen DeGeneres dropped out after a semester, and Brad Pitt quit university just 2 weeks before graduation. Even Oprah Winfrey is a university dropout, and it has not harmed her career. Richard Branson has a much higher net worth than Oprah and he too didn't even attend college, having dropped out of school at 16. The list literally goes on and on, including such icons as John Lennon, Jim Carey, Al Pacino, Wolfgang Puck, Walt Disney, Tom Hanks, Abraham Lincoln, Thomas Edison, John Henry Ford, Benjamin Franklin, Coco Chanel and Tony Robbins.

I've wondered at times what the point of a degree is, since I know many people that are successful in a field outside of their academic achievement. Art history majors aren't locked into being art gallery curators. Many of them excel in industries that have nothing at all to do with art. How is that possible you might wonder? To me, the degree proves one thing and one thing only.

Before I try to convince you what that one thing is, let's ponder for a moment the learning course of most people.

We are generally all born to parents that teach us how to behave. We are disciplined by them until school age, at which point we are given to teachers who might impose the disciplinary method of detention to keep us in line. After that, we progress to college where, if we have self-discipline, we get to graduate. Some prefer to enter the heavily disciplined armed forces and some disciplined people succeed as self-employed entrepreneurs. If you have a degree, the one thing it proves, is that you have the discipline to succeed at something difficult that takes a while to accomplish. A degree, regardless of its nature, is ultimately a measure of your self-discipline, whether that comes easily to you, or whether you must nurture the skill. Every one of the college and high school dropouts that I've brought to your attention had the self-discipline to overcome the odds. They were all successful because they were all determined to be successful.

DEFYING THE ODDS

36

Planning on accidentally becoming successful is not a good idea, and I'm not suggesting that you leave school prematurely and launch yourself into the world without a plan. To illustrate that point, did you know that there have been quite a few people in history that have survived falling out of an airplane without a parachute? Falling six miles high from the sky at 12,000 feet a minute without a parachute to break your fall is definitely not recommended, even though more than a dozen people have done it.

Those that survived, survived by accident. Deep snow landings or falling into swamps or water were responsible for their death defying feats but doing it on purpose would be irresponsible. You have a 0.0007% chance of dying from a parachute jump, but those odds go up exponentially if you say "no" to wearing a parachute. To put it another way, that's a 99.9993% chance of jumping out again if you are looking to improve your skydiving skills.

Unlike falling from a plane without a parachute, most dreams you could attempt to realize will probably afford you a second or third attempt if things don't go as hoped the first time. Actually, you'll have endless chances to try again if you are serious about your commitment. If your last diet failed, you do not have to go back to binging on pasta, pork rinds and cake. Giving up on your dreams quickly is certainly the most efficient way of failing, but if you really, really want something, not giving up is a much better idea to entertain in your head. Instead of succumbing to naysayers, including your own negative thoughts, you really could consider tapping into some of that natural brilliance that resides deep within every single one of us. We are all capable of much more than we currently realize.

We all have the capacity to imagine things going badly or to imagine things going incredibly well. All the visionaries I've mentioned have been lifted into the giddy heights of exceptional success, because they all held onto their big dreams and dismissed those who told them it could not be done. All of them have utilized methods for visualizing their aspirations and goals as possible and within reach, and some of them have gone as far as to label those methods as self-hypnosis. Personally, I like the term "High-Performance Self-Programming" because it doesn't conjure up cultural concerns about being controlled. It does what it says on the tin and doesn't press the same kind of buttons in people's heads that the word "hypnosis" can.

The word "hypnosis" is just a word. Parents pass their cultural beliefs down to us and teachers teach us what *they* were taught by *their* teachers. But, words change meaning over time as cultures and languages evolve. It could just as easily have been called "Ultra-Learning", "Mega-Focus" or "Mind-Tapping". Whatever self-hypnosis is or is isn't, it is my belief, and the belief of many of my peers in the motivational speaking and executive coaching field today, that the highly successful have all hypnotized themselves into rising to the top. In this book we will look at lots of different forms of self-hypnosis technologies, not all of which everyone will agree are hypnotic, but it just might be that any time your mind has been changed, you've been hypnotized!

DO WHATEVER IT TAKES

Each of those mega-successful people, even the academic dropouts, have followed some kind of disciplined process to hone their minds to accomplish the dreams they held dear to their hearts. They have all felt compelled to succeed, and they have all nurtured their natural talents. If you could go back in time and ask each of them what their plans were, they'd all be able to tell you the goals that they were targeting. High achievers know what they want and can tell you exactly what they are planning on achieving this week, this quarter and this year.

Your average person typically cannot do that. Ask them what their goals are, and their eyes will typically glaze over, or they'll make excuses to justify why they don't need a plan. Many people are content to be a leaf in the wind, blown wherever the breeze takes them. But those of us focused on achieving more than the average person, are far more in touch with our goals. It is crucial to have well-defined goals to focus on if you want to achieve success. If you are going to propel yourself into making any kind of impact, an unguided missile with no real target to aim at can be far worse than a leaf in the wind!

The mega-successful people I've mentioned so far didn't keep what they wanted to achieve a secret just in case they failed. They were planning to win races, win games, and break records. They had dreams to break into the film business, rise to the top of their industry and become the extraordinary individual they saw possible for them to become. They all had a clear vision of their ideal future to aim at, and they all did something about it. They were not vague about their dream, nor were they lackadaisical about making their dream into a reality. They had a plan to follow and they were not too lazy to implement it. Every single one of them built their self-belief into an unstoppable powerhouse of propulsion that eventually became second nature to them. They have each made it look easy—and for you, it can be.

If you are planning to follow in the footsteps of someone that has succeeded with what you really want to accomplish, you'll need a plan to follow. But, you probably aren't the person to invent it. Why reinvent the same wheel that has already moved others along rapidly in their endeavours? You might not be the right person to create the methodology, but you are definitely the right person to tailor it to suit your specific needs. You have the capacity to prove that what has worked for others, cannot fail at working for you.

By reverse-engineering the behaviours and techniques of the most successful people who have achieved something similar to the outcome you covet, you can avoid a tonne of time-wasting and energy-draining mistakes. You just need to diligently model their success generating strategies until you ultimately succeed too. Of course, you aren't destined to be a mega-success on day one, but with some direction and drive, and a good dose of dedication and determination (aka discipline), you might be surprised at what is possible when you really set your mind on it. There is a price to pay for absolutely everything, both failure *and* success. What are you currently investing your time into achieving?

Throughout the rest of this book, we will be looking at several proven strategies that amplify your emotional attachment to succeeding, render willpower unnecessary, and will assist you in developing a plan that cannot fail. You'll find that the average person can easily learn to make the small, simple changes in their life that help them go from ordinary to exceptional with just a little effort.

Now, of all the obstacles that might stand in your way of becoming better at what you do or learning a new skill that leads you into a more amazing life, doubt is the one thing you really need to destroy. I don't want you doubting yourself. I <u>really</u> don't want you doubting what I'm telling you. To help you eradicate any lingering doubt entirely, bear with me for a chapter while I "get all scientific" on you. But first, let's have a brief review of this chapter:

CHAPTER 2 SUMMARY

AKA:

WHAT YOU'VE LEARNED BY READING THIS CHAPTER

1. There are always at least two sides to everything in a three-dimensional universe, so you are not unilaterally defined by your genes.

2. Excellence is a mindset, not a qualification. It's learned by experience and expressed in discipline, not by reading words in a book.

3. Hypnosis is simply an absorbed learning state of receptivity and responsiveness to ideas, which works best when your mind is open to it working.

4. High-performers effectively "hypnotize" themselves to perform at a high level, even if their methods differ slightly or they don't call it self-hypnosis.

5. The easiest route is the path formed by those ahead of you, so don't reinvent the wheel – do what they do!

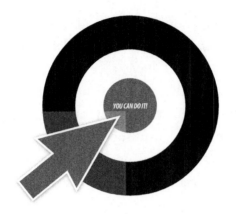

THE SCIENCE OF SUCCESS

AKA

THE REALITY OF WHO YOU ARE

Doubts are a natural part of any human experience. Relative certainty only comes from experience, and some courage is required to act on a new endeavour, even if you feel prepared. Anything new to us is unfamiliar, and a certain degree of uncertainty is part of the price you pay for getting out of your comfort zone. Comfort zones are comfortable. No-one likes constant changes unless they are a baby racing though diapers. We have the capacity to make decisions to do something different, even if it means uprooting our old mindset and implanting new ideas, that take time for us to grow comfortable with.

But, some people feel stuck in their place and unable to move forward in their life. That mindset is ridiculous, since we always have a choice. Always. Having a choice to move is the entire point of having a brain. In psychology we know this, thanks to animal studies. Animals might not be identical to human beings, but they are mammals. Plants are rooted and cannot decide to move because they do not have a brain like mammals. If you are a plant planted in the shade, you are not going to thrive unless shade is the perfect environment for the kind of flora or fauna you are. Plants in scorching sunlight can experience the opposite problem but the solution that eludes them remains the same: move! A human animal can desire the sun or the shade and make a mental decision to change their place and act on it. Deciding to move is what your brain exists to do and how that happens is deceptively simple.

Your brain is divided into two hemispheres: Left Brain and Right Brain. Although there is some overlap of functionality (like the way your hands can do the same things) there is a degree of specialization associated with each side (like the way right-handed people tend to write with their right hand and turn pages with their left). Each hemisphere of the brain controls the opposite arm. A right-handed person's left hemisphere specializes in language and thinking while the other hemisphere controls emotion and touch. This is why you might be inclined to follow the words you are reading with your right index finger, while you feel for the page to turn with your left.

Here is where things get fun: emotion contains the word MOTION in it. In the physical realm, it is not the *thought* of being too hot or too cold that moves us, it is the feeling of discomfort caused by the sensation that motivates us to move. Emotion is what drives us to do things, but only if we do not experience a conflictual thought in words, convincing us that it is not possible to do, or that we shouldn't do it. Human intellect is a powerful influence over us, but generally only as a quick fact-checker to make sure we aren't moving towards the sun and ignoring some fatal trap along the path.

All communication involves both intent and interpretation. A sign for FREE DRINKS TODAY might intend to motivate patrons to enter a bar, but if we are on the way to work, we might need to remind ourselves of our professional responsibilities and decide to ignore the sign or come back to it later. If you want to keep your job, you may need to interpret the message as not for you, or at least not right now. This might feel patronizing to read, but some work might need to get done before you clock off and reward yourself by relaxing over a beer or a martini after your work day is done.

Luxury car ads aren't concerned with pointing out the pitfalls of a long-term high-interest loan on a degradable product, or the practicality of a car that can go 200 miles/hour on a highway with a maximum speed limit of 55 miles/hour. They are primarily appealing to the emotions of the prospective new car owner who would love to feel like the powerful owner of a performance automobile. Decisions to purchase prestige vehicles are generally based on imagination and emotion, not sense or practicality. Your right brain generates emotions and your left brain attempts to make sense of it, not the other way around.

Words and ideas pop into your conscious awareness, but they are not created there. Creativity comes from the emotional right brain, not the seat of logic and reason. Essentially, you are driven by your unconscious, illogical and emotional right brain, not the logical left hemisphere, where you derive your sense of being in conscious control. When you can't make conscious sense of your unconscious feeling, you might find yourself stuck in a conflictual bind. Like a smoker attempting to quit smoking because of what they know about the harms and dangers of smoking, feeling compelled to light up again by the relief they imagine it will bring them to stop withholding from themselves the experience they crave. Or someone craving sleep but making it difficult for themselves by entertaining worrying thoughts about insomnia. My job as a speaker, coach and trainer, is to help human beings break the stalemate that has been locking them into their problem.

Thanks to neuroscience, the old adage that "you cannot teach an old dog new tricks" has been blown out of the water, at least when it comes to human beings. Neuroplasticity is the term for our ability to generate new neurological pathways, or habits. We may have many conditioned habits in our "hardwiring", but a considerable degree of rewiring remains a possibility for us if we want to make a small change, or even a significant change.

There was a time when we didn't understand the fundamental flaws inherent in remembering (aka putting our memories back together). Substantial evidence has been collected that clearly shows how vulnerable memories are being distorted and manipulated. However, we can use that knowledge to our advantage when redesigning our lives. We can decide to purposefully influence our own memory banks by adding imaginatively rehearsed experiences into our own neurology, because at some level our brains cannot discern the difference between what was real, what was dreamed, and what was vividly imagined.

The part of our brain that separates us from other mammals is the prefrontal lobe. It is the decision-making part of us that can weigh up the emotion and logic, and decide what action is best for us, despite any downsides that may accompany it. Fear of getting trapped might motivate an animal not to take some juicy bait, but dogs cannot decide to teach themselves new tricks. We can.

Dogs learn by pleasure and pain, just like we do. But, we can set out to purposefully override a crippling fear when we set our mind to it. With the right techniques, it's a simple matter to change your own brain's programming. You can think of it as "self-directed neuroplasticity" if you like.

YOUR BRAIN IS A COMPUTER

Our bihemispheric brain codes even the most complex information in simple binary terms. It is the most powerful organic computer on the planet. But even the most powerful manmade computer with the most complicated userinterface, is still coded at its basic level in binary. One or zero, yes or no, on or off.

For us, the binary system extends to an infinite number of opposites, including: like or dislike, friend or foe, enemy or ally, love or hate, dark or light, hot or cold, mobile or immobile, do or don't, can or cannot, wrong or right, true or false, near or far, towards or away, new or familiar, you or me, them or us, up or down, bad or good, fat or thin, long or short, possible or impossible, danger or safety, rigid or flexible, hard or soft, left or right, rich or poor, succeed or fail, sink or swim, etc. Each binary pair has a learned association with pleasure or pain, which either lures us towards or repels us away from either pole on each continuum.

American psychologist Edward Thorndike's law of effect is a psychological principle that furthered the emerging field of behavioural conditioning back in 1898. The law of effect states that **any event or response followed by a pleasurable consequence, will tend to be repeated. If an event or response is followed by an unpleasant consequence, it will tend to be avoided.** He proved his theory by experimenting on cats trapped in a puzzling box that had to learn to find their way out in order to get a fishy reward.

Regardless how you feel about scientists stressing cats out in a lab, his theory holds true today and we can use it to our advantage when training ourselves to develop effective habits. We'll be exploring how to use self-conditioning methods in a later chapter, but for now, I hope it's clear that the polar opposite sensations of pleasure and pain (aka reward and punishment) are the fundamental references for all experiences, and not just for felines.

OPPOSING POLES

We process everything in the dualistic terms of opposites even though there are gradients between dark and light, like the grey area between black and white. We tip the balance by focusing more or less on one side or the other. Where you place your focus counts. We don't always see the inbetween, especially when we are under psychological pressure. Our brains are primarily programmed to keep us safe, and when you are suddenly put in a high-pressure situation, there is no time to think.

Picture this scenario: you are crossing the road when you become aware that an oncoming car has run the red light and the car is about to hit you. Proximity is a critical aspect of emotionally driven motivation. Instincts to move kick in before we can take the time to ponder whether to jump or step forwards, sideways or backwards. If the vehicle is far away, we are less motivated to make an immediate move. Instead, we might just think about it for a while. A vehicle could stop, or make a turn before it reaches us, so it is inefficient to worry about it too much ahead of time. When the car gets dangerously close, you'll feel much more motivated to make a move.

Time restrictions can be effective motivators. Stress your mind out with a dangerous deadline and your brain defaults to "black and white thinking". Relax it with more time, and your mind can open to the full spectrum of possibilities that also exist. It takes a lot of processing power to be in a perpetual state of considering *everything*, so our efficiency-seeking organic computer thrives on the habit-forming process of pattern matching. "If it looks like a duck it is probably a duck," your brain immediately reasons, "and if it looks like danger, it is probably dangerous." Sometimes we can be tricked by decoys, but that's just one of the perils of not taking the time to process properly. If something looks difficult to achieve, it might be. But if we take the time to really assess the situation, we often find that what we want to accomplish might be a lot easier than we imagined.

Your binary brain processes pleasure and pain and instinctively moves you towards what is good and away from what is expected to be bad. You will feel drawn in the direction of pleasant pleasure or repelled away from unpleasant pain. Your brain uses the two branches of your nervous system, the sympathetic and the parasympathetic, to provoke or pacify you by triggering a stress response or a relaxation response. The chemistry created will cause you to experience either tension or relief, and what you feel is greatly dependent on your expectation of the experience.

Near is more compelling than far, and sooner is far more compelling than later. That is how credit card companies can get you to reward yourself with what you want right now, leaving the bill as a delayed consequence a month off in the distance. If you did stop to think about whether you could easily afford the repayments or not, it would significantly influence your decision to make the purchase or put it back on the shelf.

Pain is unpleasant to think about, and determined shoppers often push it out of their minds as they reward themselves _right now_, regardless of the cost to them later. Let's face the facts: when you desperately want to make a change in your life, some kind of pain is, ultimately, the price of failure. All change involves some stress. If you are determined to only feel relaxed and good, you may have mindlessly rewarded yourself with the relief of giving up _in the present_, rather than risk the potential of failure that could result from trying.

Humans are chemical beings and all the emotions we experience are chemically delivered by chemical messengers called neurotransmitters. The neuroscientist that discovered the human opiate receptor and the binding site for endorphins, Candace Pert calls them the molecules of emotion – and so motion really does come from emotion. Every impulse is the result of chemistry regulated by your brain via the nervous system. Staying safe feels good because it is a chemical wash of "good feeling" biochemistry. The reward you can experience by purposefully failing (aka giving up), is a chemical reward of pleasing relief. The price you pay however, is being unsuccessful. If that does not result in unpleasant consequences, you'll probably rationalize being ok with how things are.

IT'S EASY TO KEEP GOING ONCE YOU GET STARTED

Newton's First Law of Motion informs us that "a body in motion stays in motion unless acted upon by an equal and opposite force". Apples fall to the ground unless stopped by something strong enough stop an apple. Runaway trains keep going and going unless something stronger than a train gets in its way or someone slams on powerful brakes. By a similar logic, "if you want something doing, you ask a busy person". Busy people are already in motion and it takes them less energy to accomplish a new task than a lethargic person lazing on a couch. A body lying on a couch stays lying on a couch unless acted upon by a powerful force. Yell "Fire!" or set fire to the couch, and they might get up to avoid the burning pain. Offer them a pile of gold bullion to "get the hell up!" and they just might take those karats and also avoid being berated.

| The Carrot | The Stick |
| Compelled towards | Propelled away |

We respond to rewards and punishments, whether they are externally offered to us, or internally generated (like the rewards of accomplishment and relief, respectively). We are also motivated by the punishments of incompetence and feeling like a loser. Regardless of how many times you've tried and failed at succeeding, you are not defined by your past memories. **You are defined by the memories you make today.** Please read that last sentence again louder in your head.

Returning to neuroscience: thanks to Hebb's Law (which states that the connections between two neurons is strengthened when both neurons are fired simultaneously), we in the business of change understand that "what fires together, wires together." People with a phobia of dogs may have developed a "wired-in" fear of dogs by experiencing one or two strong reactions in the presence of an angry neighbourhood dog. But that in no way means that all dogs are scary. A few highly positive experiences in the presence of happy gentle dogs and their wiring could quite easily change if they were open to it. Of course, those positive experiences need to accumulate an emotion as strong as the phobic fear, but thanks to the reality that many dogs are far from scary, this is possible.

Habits of thinking, feeling, perceiving and responding, are all open to some rewiring with the right experiences. Anyone in sales or sports who has experienced some scary prospects or a few bad performances, could be forgiven for assuming that they've lost their "mojo".

They haven't lost their mojo, they've accidentally programmed in a success-defeating expectancy of failure. To paraphrase Einstein, "You cannot solve a problem with the same mindset that created it". We are state-dependent learners. If we are in a particular state when we learn something, we will associate that state to the learning. The implication of this, is that if you have a habit of misunderstanding something, you aren't likely to spontaneously realize your error unless someone else points it out to you, or you are somehow able to consider it from a different state than misunderstanding.

Spend time around dogs while in a state of fear and the state and stimulus will wire together in your brain. Be relaxed around dogs (a different state) and different neurons wire together. Be calm around dogs often, and the wiring gets stronger and harder to break to the point where it would be hard to convince you that dogs are not man's best friend. Repetition burns in neurological connections, and strong emotions supercharge the process.

If you currently love apples but experience an apple so bad that you become sick for a week, you might start to doubt your love of apples. Suffer a few more poisonous, rancid apples, and you might just decide you no longer like them.

It doesn't matter whether apples are generally good or not, any more than the reality of dogs factors into the equation. It is YOUR emotional reality of dogs or apples that dictates YOUR neurological habit pattern, regardless of what anyone else's intellect tries to convince you. A few emotional, strongly wired responses to the stimulus of dog or apple and you'll understand that practice doesn't really make perfect. In reality, practice makes permanent.

PRACTICE MAKES PERMANENT

Practice the wrong notes on the piano and your unconscious will learn the wrong notes perfectly. Mindlessly run through the tune and you'll keep making the same mistakes over and over again.

Once you've wired some memories together, disconnecting them becomes a challenge, although not an impossible one. Thankfully, we respond to rewards, and if they are fairly immediate, we will pair the rewarding feeling with the behaviour that we'd like to make automatic.

If you got a passionate kiss from your favourite celebrity every time you: played the right note on the keyboard; chose an apple over a chocolate bar; or made a cold call that you've been dreading, it would accelerate your relearning process. Zap you with a mini taser each time you played a wrong note, and you'd be a highly motivated to improve very quickly. If you are motivated to avoid the pain of that shock and get the pleasure of that celebrity smooch, woe betide anyone that gets in your way! Don't believe me? Just watch a TV show about extreme stalkers or drug addicts and see what lengths they'll go to for the possibility of being near their celebrity obsession or to finally get their fix.

Well, I've got news for you. We all entertain some obsessions and we are all addicts of one kind or another. You are an addict because all good experiences elicit good chemistry, even if the chemicals are not illicit or considered bad for you. The main chemicals I'm referring to are Serotonin, Noradrenaline and the granddaddy of chemical rewards: Dopamine (why do you think they call it "dope"?). All three are powerful mood regulators and all three play a part in getting and staying motivated.

Serotonin is basically our happy chemical. Noradrenaline (aka Norepinephrine to those in the U.S) is responsible for arousal, and dopamine grabs our attention. Together dopamine and noradrenaline create a chemical cocktail of attention intensity which plays a massive part in creating lasting change. No dog phobic ever learned that dogs are vicious and frightening by ignoring snarling, snapping dogs playing dangerously near them.

If you are like most western workers, you are probably addicted to your smartphone to some degree. You've probably had the experience of waiting at a red light (that you've learned to associate with stopping) and wondered if you got any texts or emails. If you checked your phone, you are an addict. Whether you got a message or not, you got a little burst of dopamine reward that felt somewhat better than the twinge of anxious uncertainty that made you check your phone. You escaped the stick of not knowing and cashed in on the carrot of certainty. Mild though it may have been, your desire to end anxiety and get an immediately gratifying reward of knowing, was the motivation that being a slave to technology has conditioned you with.

If you ever found yourself so engrossed in reading a message on your phone that you did not notice the traffic light had gone green, you probably got a wakeup call from the horn of the car behind you that snapped you out of your trance and got you moving again. In the moments before your rude awakening, dopamine will have locked your attention and blocked your awareness of the changing signals. Adrenaline might get you going, but noradrenaline is what keeps you motivated to move.

My aim in writing this book is that I might just be able to wake you up from whatever self-defeating trance you could be in and motivate you into a more satisfying state of being and doing better.

It's a scientific fact that emotions are brief and fleeting. Fifteen seconds or so is about the length of time an emotional burst lasts in our nervous system. If you feel good, it doesn't last long, but you can fire-off subsequent bursts, by throwing fuel on the flash-fire. Even bad feelings like anxiety (aka anticipatory fear) are over within moments, unless you continue to imagine terrible things in your mind or worry yourself with alarming words in your head. Our feelings stimulate motion. Motivating or demotivating thoughts and ideas fuel our emotions. It's a cycle that you can break if you decide to. The cycle does not have to be vicious, it can be very friendly indeed.

We can trigger good feelings with pleasant tastes and smells. Grandma's apple pie can appeal to our gustatory sense of taste and our olfactory sense of smell. But of our five known senses, the three primary pathways that highly successful people tend to use to program or reprogram themselves (without gaining weight), are:

THE 3 PRIMARY PATHWAYS TO SELF-PROGRAMMING

1. **VISUAL** (sight)

2. **AUDITORY** (sound) and

3. **KINAESTHETIC** (tactile sensations and feelings)

No one ever got fat listening to a self-help sound-file, watching a motivational video, or feeling a sense of accomplishment or reward. Watching the food channel and hearing how mindbogglingly great double-bypass burgers are, might motivate some people into breaking their healthy eating habit. You must be selective in what you expose your senses to, and not just because your senses inform you about the world around you.

What you see and hear affects how you feel. What you feel determines what you do. That doesn't just apply to sights and sounds processed from outside. We all have an inner ear and a mind's eye, just like we feel tactile sensations from outside and emotional feelings from within. What you say to yourself in your own head, and how you see yourself in your mind's eye, are even more important. Because even when you are daydreaming, or fully asleep, your mind is processing your inner world. Your inner world forms the person you believe yourself to be, the person that is interacting with the outside world.

It might seem silly to some, but if you've had an experience in the past that has made you believe that you are someone that doesn't like clowns, then whenever you see a clown or hear a clown's honking horn, you are not going to enjoy the experience. Clowns have no inherent quality to them, only people's differing opinions about them based on what they were told about clowns or whether their first experience of clowns was funny or scary. If you are freaked out by the idea of clowns, your brain will be on the lookout for clowns so that you can avoid them. If you love them, you will also be on the lookout for them at some level. No particular feeling about clowns? You probably won't even notice them.

Your brain's primary role is the survival of you (the home it lives in). You are going to notice things to avoid because your brain learns by experience what to alert you to. You'll also be alerted to tasty things, and sexy stuff because you are preprogrammed to eat and procreate so that you and your species can survive. Now there is a ridiculous amount of sights, sounds and smells around you, much of which you are unaware of. Your unconscious mind is processing millions of bits of data every moment, but thanks to cognitive psychologist George Miller's research in the 50's, we know that at any given time, you can only be consciously aware of around 7 things (+/− 2). Some more recent studies strongly suggest that we can only be aware of one thing at a time!

YOUR RETICULAR ACTIVATING SYSTEM

When you pool your attention and narrow your focus, everything else drops out of awareness unless it grabs your attention. With all the sensoria around you, your awareness is greatly limited by a filtering process that takes place in the base of your brain stem. Of all the stimulating data that your unconscious mind is tracking constantly, your Reticular Activating System (RAS) determines what pops into your consciousness. First and foremost, are the things pertinent to your survival that take precedence. After that, anything you've impressed upon your brain to watch out for will be permitted to pass through the funnel. If you close your eyes at the end of this paragraph and say only the word "RED, RED, RED" urgently over and over to yourself for about 30-60 seconds, then on opening your eyes, rapidly scan your environment, you might be surprised how easy it is to prove this to yourself. Ok, go....

Chances are, when you opened your eyes and moved your head quickly from left to right and from top to bottom, your eyes were drawn to anything red in your field of vision. Your RAS prioritizes your awareness, and it learns *what* to prioritize from you. What you notice is a by-product of what you desire to see. Remember the hero of Martin Handford's books? Do you want to find where Waldo is? Ask yourself "Where's Waldo, Waldo, Waldo?" and finding him amongst the crowd will be way easier. Want to notice the healthy options on a menu, or the signs of a motivated prospect ready to buy? You just have to program your brain to bring them into your attention.

A fascinating experiment that illustrates the difference between those that consider themselves lucky and those that don't, has shown us that it comes down to the opportunities they notice. Self-diagnosed "unlucky" people don't easily or automatically register unscratched lottery tickets when they are purposefully left in their path. "Lucky" people do notice them and have a greater expectation of good fortune programmed into their neurology.

WHAT ARE YOU FOCUSED ON?

In business and in life, the opportunities you notice will be highly dependent on your expectations. If you expect to have a difficult day at the office, your RAS will be filtering up all the evidence you need to feel justified in having a poor outlook. Our brains do not like to be wrong and go to great lengths to prove us right. Optimism and pessimism are learned habits of thinking and awareness—and learned habits can be unlearned. Habits can be broken and rebuilt on purpose, with persistence.

Some people get stuck in the habit of buying lottery tickets because they delusionally expect to win. That faulty expectation fires off a dopamine reward that tricks them into feeling a false sense of accomplishment. If I wanted to get rich, I wouldn't plan on getting rich by a stroke of luck, I'd suggest doing things that make it far more likely.

The harder you work, the luckier you'll get, as long as you are working at the right thing. You make your own success in life, but it does help to notice the opportunities along the way. I wouldn't put my faith in a lottery and I wouldn't worry much about getting struck by lightning unless I was standing outside on a hill next to a tall tree in a lightning storm. Then, I might need to quickly become aware of my precarious position and make a quick move in the right direction. As a final thought before moving on to the next chapter, scan your eyes rapidly over the following word search puzzles and make note of the first word or two that you become aware of. There are 15 positive words and 15 negative words in each word search for you to notice. You'll get to see what your RAS selects to show you first. Then you'll know whether your brain is primed and programmed to process the positive or negative when it comes to the idea of succeeding.

WHAT DO YOU SEE FIRST?

```
B C A C H I E V E F E A R T L
M Y X S E D A N G E R J S R O
F I G H T C O N F L I C T E V
W T L T H O P E L E S S U X E
F R O Z E N P G M N T T C C W
E I S G F T O A P J R R K I I
F C E A E R R T O O A E F T N
F H R M J O T I S Y T S O I N
I A D E S L U V I K E S C N E
C T O H T N N E T X G V U G R
I E U U V K I W I J Y M S Q T
E Q B W M O T I V A T E D I J
N M T E R X Y D E L E A O X E
C O N F I D E N T F L I G H T
Y P R A C T I C A L H I D E Z
```

WHAT DO YOU SEE FIRST?

```
C R E A T E C P O S S I B L E
R E F U S E F F I C I E N C Y
M O E C R E L A X A T I O N E
P U R S U E D O N D P A N I C
E X C E L L E N C E F I G H T
G H O P E I M P O S S I B L E
R A M A Z E O B S T A C L E A
R E F U S E T E R R I F I E D
L S C W T T I G R O W P A O D
A U K O L N V X O Y R L M B I
C C N U I R A W J L E A A U C
T C S W D L T B A N J C Z R T
R E P L A C E A B L E E I D I
R E S I S T D D C M C B N E O
O D I F F I C U L T T O G N N
```

POSITIVE	NEGATIVE
1. EFFICIENCY	1. HOPELESS
2. RICH	2. INEFFICIENCY
3. WINNER	3. LOSER
4. EXCITING	4. DANGER
5. CONFIDENT	5. ANXIETY
6. FIGHT	6. STRESS
7. LOVE	7. FLIGHT
8. MOTIVATED	8. STUCK
9. OPPORTUNITY	9. FROZEN
10. POSSIBLE	10. FEAR
11. CONTROL	11. FIGHT
12. ACHIEVE	12. CONFLICT
13. STRATEGY	13. DOUBT
14. PRACTICAL	14. HATE
15. FOCUS	15. BAD
16. GAME	16. ADDICTION
17. ENJOY	17. DEMOTIVATED
18. HOPE	18. BURDEN
19. PLACEBO	19. DESTROY
20. RELAXATION	20. OBSTACLE
21. CREATE	21. IMPOSSIBLE
22. EXCELLENCE	22. REPLACEABLE
23. AMAZING	23. DIFFICULT
24. PERSIST	24. RESIST
25. PURSUE	25. REFUSE
26. GROW	26. REJECT
27. RESULT	27. RECOIL
28. WIN	28. HIDE
29. AMAZE	29. TERRIFIED
30. SUCCEED	30. PANIC

Don't worry if the words you see first are demotivating, or if you seem focused on failure. Remember, your RAS prioritizes safety first, and might bring threatening words to your immediate attention. But thanks to neuroplasticity, and the capacity for programming your RAS, you can train your brain and prime your mind to fixate on whatever you really, really want—whatever that really is? Let's ponder that now together in the next chapter, after first pointing out some of the key learnings from this one:

CHAPTER 3 SUMMARY

AKA:

WHAT YOU'VE LEARNED BY READING THIS CHAPTER

1. You can choose to improve, since your brain can always change.

2. Your emotional chemistry rules you in the forms of pain and pleasure. So focus your precious attention on the pleasure of succeeding and the price of failure, not the stress of striving to achieve more and the relief of not having to try.

3. Immediate goals that are within your reach are more compelling than distant ones beyond your grasp.

4. Formed habits become almost automatic and effortless, regardless of how they were formed.

5. In addition to survival needs, your RAS seeks out whatever you focus it on, so focus it wisely and on purpose.

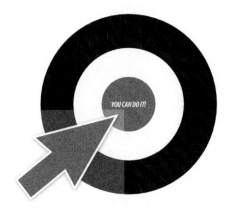

CHAPTER 4

WHAT DO YOU WANT TO SUCCEED AT?

AKA

GETTING CLEAR ABOUT YOUR MOTIVATION TO CHANGE

There is probably a great deal more to you than you are aware of, and you are definitely capable of a lot more than you might currently realize. With almost infinite possibilities in your future, the degree of clarity you currently have about your immediate steps, is going to greatly influence the outcome you can realistically expect for yourself.

How you feel about turning your dreams into reality will factor in heavily. Good is pleasant, pleasurable and rewarding. Bad is unpleasant, painful and punishing. Whatever you focus on will affect you, since "affect" is a clinical term for emotion, and emotions let you know about your experience of living, as well as moving you in life.

We are driven by desire, emotion creating motion. Emotive forces motivate our movements. Feelings motivating action and action mobilizing feelings. Having a big juicy dream to salivate over is going to whet your appetite when it comes to making a move in the direction of your goal. You might not know all the possible obstacles in advance of setting off, but if you've got your sights firmly set on a desirable destination, you won't immediately give up if you hit an obstacle or get sent on a detour or two. Simply put, when you know **why** you are doing something important to you, then you will overcome any **how.**

If getting a good night's sleep is important to you, it will be easy to turn the TV off, shut down the laptop, put down your book, or end the phone call to your sister when it's time to focus on sleeping. Some people routinely lay in bed ruminating about their day, or spending the time worrying about tomorrow. It's possible to let your brain wander wherever it wants and wonder whatever it likes. But, being a good brain owner is like being a good dog owner. You must focus it effectively, teach it how to behave and you shouldn't reward it for bad behaviour.

If you want to fall asleep, you are much better off pooling all of your attention onto aspects that are conducive to falling asleep, rather than entertaining any stressful thoughts. Do not invest energy into anything stimulating, worrying, or in any way counterproductive to sleeping. Don't think-think-think to yourself about how hard it is to fall asleep and you won't feel-

feel-feel threatened by the thought that you might be awake all night. The only difference between someone with insomnia and someone without insomnia, is that the person without insomnia doesn't wonder if they'll be able to sleep tonight!

Want to succeed at sleeping? Focus on the coolness of the soft pillow. Pretend your body is already asleep and notice how nice the comforter feels, wrapped around you like a baby being swaddled. If the idea of that makes you think claustrophobic thoughts, stop that! It's a blanket, not a locked cupboard! It's easy to imagine anything with your eyes closed, so be careful with what you do imagine, since it's going to impact your state of being. Positive or negative, whatever thoughts you give your attention to will magnify in your mind.

Don't fertilize a bad idea with terrible thoughts, because wherever your attention goes, energy grows. A tightrope walker inching their way between two skyscraping rooftops without a net, is safer focusing exclusively on the opposite end of the rope, rather than the infinite number of places where they could fall to their demise.

To put that into a business perspective: Multi-million-dollar property developers are aware that there are risks involved with every transaction. But if they focused on all the ways that the deal could go bad, instead of on the good outcome that they are aiming for, many of them would leave their net worth in safe bonds, locked into low rates of interest and safe from the real estate market crashing. The potential gains *and* the potential risks will always go hand in hand in any endeavour, work, play or otherwise. So, risk only what you are prepared to lose and then only focus on the returns, neither of which need be money.

MONEY CAN'T BUY ME LOVE

Money for the sake of money is not as exciting as some people might think. What you can spend money on however, can be incredibly motivating. The experience of an early morning dip in your hotel's heated indoor pool is probably way more satisfying than owning a pool that you never swim in could ever be. The feeling of being debt-free might be preferable to the feeling of being indebted to some bank, for the privilege of owning a home with so many rooms that you can avoid sleeping in the same bed twice in any given week.

Money is a means to an end, not the be all and end all of anything. It's a commonly accepted sign of success, but it is not THE sign of success. Be sure to focus your long-range aspirations on an experience that would make you feel successful once you have achieved it. Maybe having mid-morning brunches on your Malibu beach house deck? Or jetting off to Aspen for the weekend to ski with celebrities? A real hunger for success comes from knowing why you want it. So be sure to be honest with yourself about your true motivation, and that motivation will be easy to amplify and multiply.

Life is not an acquisition, life is an experience. Therefore, you should invest in the experience that you'll be glad you had when your last day comes. Your experience of life is an entirely subjective experience that only you alone can ever truly appreciate. You get to choose what kind of experience you want from your life, and trust me, it is not the trophy, but what it feels like to be awarded the trophy that matters most. A gold medal winner could lose, sell or even auction off their medal, and still not lose the feeling that they were, are, and always will be, a gold medal winner. The medal is only a symbol of the winning spirit within.

Accomplishments can be very satisfying, and satisfaction leads to happiness. Trying to buy happiness is as hopeless as trying to buy love. It cannot be done. The sense of satisfaction is a subjective feeling that also cannot be bought. It can however be earned. Satisfaction comes from the sense of achieving something worthwhile. It does not come from frustration or failure, and the easiest way to experience those foul feelings is to take on too much or bite off more than you can chew. Attempt too much, and the probability of failure increases.

I'm not condoning eating the elephant in the room, but if you were to give it a go, I highly recommend not trying to digest the entire beast in one sitting! Small, manageable mouthfuls are the way to go, and don't expect to be done any time soon. Big goals can take a while. Impatience and unrealistic expectations are not conducive to maintaining motivation. Negative feelings come from negative experiences, and if we become overwhelmed by the enormity of it all, we are not going to inspire the frame of mind needed to keep going.

When it comes to achieving something incredible and awe inspiring, breaking the big goal down into some small, reasonable steps is going to help you immensely. Small practical steps promote success. Your big goal can be mammoth, but you shouldn't put more on your plate than you are happy to devour. Make yourself sick of struggling today, and you'll probably find an excuse to avoid having to struggle through another serving tomorrow.

BIG JUICY GOAL

The first step is to figure out what you want. What you really, really want. And just as importantly, why? Your long-term mega-goal should be inspiring and can even be somewhat out of reach. If you can get it easily now, then it's a short-term goal. A good long-term goal is something awaiting you as a reward for your continued daily efforts. Thinking three to five years in the future might be a realistic time frame. Or, you might have a more manageable one – to two – year goal—as long as you aren't being overzealous and unrealistic about how quickly it is possible, you get to set the timeframe you'll be working with.

Let's look at the kinds of long term goals you might wish to entertain.

THE SIX CATEGORIES OF LONG-TERM GOALS:

6. Personal / Hobby

5. Relational / Romantic

4. Community / Environmental

3. Financial / Investment

2. Business / Work

1. Wellness / Health

These align with Abraham Maslow's hierarchy of needs. I have divided these into six categories. Maslow divided the developmental striving of human beings into five levels of needs, arranged from most basic at the foundation, to advanced needs at the pinnacle. He advised that you shouldn't focus on higher levels of change if you do not have your foundational levels in place and functional. The order isn't rigid, but wellness comes first since if you do not have that, you are somewhat hobbled in everything else.

Maslow's five levels leading to self-actualization require your **physical needs** be met first: food, water, warmth and rest, but none more important than breathing. Next is your **safety and**

security: a home, a strong healthy body, money and insurance. Followed by **social needs**: belonging, love, intimacy, relationships and sex. That all in place, the focus can effectively move up to **self-esteem** related concepts: being valued, achievements, personal interests, winning awards and getting appreciated. Feeling great doing things you love, for no other reason than your love of doing things, is the pinnacle.

At the pinnacle of this sustainable achievements pyramid is **self-actualization.** Maslow defined self-actualization as: **what a person can be, they must be, in order to be satisfied.** Which follows the formula: **make full use of your talents, capabilities and potential, and exploit them to your satisfaction.** At that level, the opinions of others matter little in your search for achieving your potential. Dr. Victor Frankl might argue that his book, *Man's Search for Meaning*, is evidence that someone in as dire a situation as a concentration camp, can still aspire to create, despite their circumstances. Ultimately, the right mindset will win out.

Your satisfaction is what matters. It's your choice to do what appeals to you to achieve, on one condition: that it exploits your talents, capabilities and potential. You can't efficiently focus on a high-level goal unless you have an established foundation that doesn't require much of your attention. You can't jump in the ring and be a prize fighter if you have no foundational training. Start where you need to start and focus where you need to focus first. Real contenders are contenders that earn their shot at the top, not dreamers that do nothing but dream. You won't find yourself winning the championship match by accident. Right action is essential, and some achievements require building up to.

In order that your goals become stable enough to sustain, you must focus first on the foundational steps. Either you have all the steps in place and you are going to ace a high-level goal you are ready to take aim at, or you are going to have to focus on the groundwork you'll need in place in order to get you to where you can aspire to more.

The world's first stress expert, Hans Selye, would tend to agree with Abraham Maslow. Selye didn't start out waking people up to the realities of stress. He first had to pay his dues working under the supervision of others before he was permitted to focus solely on his own scientific interests. He certainly enjoyed and appreciated the attention his work brought him, but he believed that his self-centred, self-actualizing focus on award-winning scientific research, was ultimately something with altruistic benefits. His primary motivation was to satisfy a deep need he had for approval from others, justified by the benefits it brought to mankind. His "Altruistic-Egotism" set the stage for the kind of win-win striving that comes highly endorsed by highly effective people like Stephen Covey. It's great when what you desire to achieve is good for others too!

Selye would also agree that, regardless of what you focus your energy on, there is always a price to pay. You can spend your life-energy on dissatisfying tasks and enduring an agonizing existence. Or, conversely, you can invest your precious life-energy into satisfying experiences and purposeful acquisitions that feel good to utilize. There is a stress-price to pay for everything, good or bad, and you are better off finding some way of enjoying whatever you do, if you MUST to do it.

Find a way of making whatever you are doing fun. If your big goal requires it, that's great, but if you are just enjoying activities that don't lead you closer to your end goal, you are a leaf in the wind. Yes, have fun doing nothing, but also have fun doing something at least half the time, if not more.

Selye's stress response theory has yet to be disproven by anyone. Modern science says of Maslow's funnelling of energy: that the steps aren't rigid, but they are right. My list of six are not different needs regardless that they form a different number of groupings with different labels, since there are various routes to the shared target (aka goal).

Regardless of the type of goal, they all have one thing in common: all goals benefit from having purposeful habits that support them. Anything can become a habit with the right kind of nurturing, something I'll be covering in detail in the next few chapters. It's your choice what you focus on, but make your choice wisely. Only you can decide what you really want and why. But make sure you do really want it, because you might just get it!

It isn't the goal itself that is motivating, it's imagining the experience that the goal promises, that unleashes the emotional punch needed to achieve it. Strong emotions are a heady cocktail that not only change your state, they also change your thinking. We have the capacity to act out of character when antagonized or intoxicated by potent chemistry (love, anger and angel dust as examples), even though we remain essentially who we are. We've all heard stories of an adrenalized parent with hysterical strength, lifting a crushing car off their infant child. Average though most of us may be, we are all capable of incredible things with the right motivation pulling the strings on our neurochemistry.

TALK ABOUT THE PASSION

It's paramount to make sure that you are aiming yourself at something you feel passionate about, otherwise you might quit pursuing it prematurely. In my days as a therapist, I've come across an alarming number of people that said they weren't passionate about anything. It seems they believed that passion should be obvious and known, rather than subtle and discovered.

Passion is like an awesome pair of shoes. You might know that you need a new pair of shoes, but until you spend some time trying on a few pairs in a few shoe stores or searching for shoes online, how could you possibly know which pair you were going to fall in love with? If you are not currently aware of where your passions lie, ask yourself the question: "What do I really want from life?" and patiently remain relaxed and open to realizing the answer, even if it takes some time.

If you struggle with that, you might need some advice about how to draw the answer out of your mind. (Or you might still be thinking about getting some new shoes?) Psychological research has shown that occupying your conscious mind on a task after pondering a question can keep your preprogrammed assumptions out of the way long enough for an elusive answer to be realized. Being relaxed can help too, and that's why you have so many good ideas in the shower! Science strongly suggests that you trust your subconscious mind to ponder on the answer while you take your limited conscious mind off the topic.

While I was pursuing a degree in psychology, I would routinely read the essay questions at the back of multiple-choice exams to give my subconscious mind time to figure out which topic I should invest my time writing about. I often found that my initial thoughts about which essays I wanted to write, differed from the subjects I ultimately wrote essays on. It was as if my ego was quickly picking desirable topics to write about, but by the time I'd finished answering a few hundred multiple-choice questions, it frequently dawned on me that I knew more about some less interesting essay topics that would net me a much higher grade. Of course, I made a habit of writing the essays that supported my goal of graduating rather than obeying my initial impulse! That strategy kept me in the top 10% of my classes.

This creative strategy has been proven to assist people struggling with lateral thinking exercises. It is something to consider the next time you are having trouble making decisions or seeking answers that currently elude you. That psychological technique works in the same way that a forgotten name might pop into your mind some time after wondering what their name is. Trying hard to remember will probably just constipate your cognition. Relax, and let it drop effortlessly into your mind!

YOU HAVE VALUES

Only you can know what is truly valuable to you, whether it's comfort, laughter, love, security, spontaneity, excitement, efficiency, or ecology as examples. You can have a fantastic time sleeping in different hotel rooms every month without the burden of paying the mortgage on the building. Sometimes it's better to have a friend with a boat that appreciates you bringing aboard a case of beer, then having to pay docking fees and deal with barnacles and bank loans.

Your goals must align with your specific value system as a human being if you are going to stand any chance of achieving them. It's pointless striving to become a military leader if you don't believe that anyone should ever have to be obedient to an authority, or subservient to a hierarchy. You should not dream of being a super-rich realtor that deals only with high-end clientele if you despise the wealthy and are disgusted by opulence. Choosing a big goal that is out of alignment with your deep beliefs is not a clever direction to pursue, regardless how lucrative you may imagine it to be.

MID-TERM TARGETS

After establishing your long-term goal, you'll need to get clear on which milestones along the way would be good mid-range markers. If the big goal is set for five years from now, what has to happen along the way that will lead you towards it? Your mid-range goals should be achievements that are possible within a three – to six – month period of focusing on them. Certainly, no longer than a year or two. You can always recalibrate if you find yourself getting off track. But without thinking about the territory you will need to pass through to get where you are headed, your big goal will probably just stay a big dream.

If your dream is to own and fly your own private plane, your mid-term goals might include getting your pilot's license and accruing a significant sum in your bank account. If you'd like to become the biggest selling realtor in your office so that you can look forward to an early retirement, you might need to double your property sales over the next couple of years or quadruple the number of open houses you host. Dream of earning a PhD? You might need to set your sights on a master's degree first.

The big goal doesn't always need to be entirely achievable. It's often better to aim for the moon and end up in the stars, than not setting your sights anywhere. But these mid-range stepping stones benefit greatly from being entirely doable, even if you cannot realize them today. Every big juicy goal needs some closer targets to hit first. Those mid-range goals don't just happen. They, too, have smaller steps that lead you to them. As salesman and motivational speaker Zig Ziglar was famous for saying, "No one ever accidentally found themselves at the top of Mount Everest".

The Game of Life

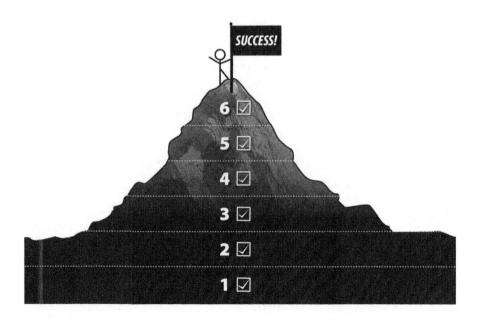

SMALL SIMPLE STEPS

It's one thing to want to make more house sales or lose weight, but if you are not increasing your client base, or decreasing your food intake, it really is unlikely to happen. Small tangible steps and short-range goals provoke the immediate actions that bring mid-range targets into view. You might not yet see the significant results of your efforts, but you can probably tell if you are doing what is needed or not by the milestones you meet or miss.

How much less do you need to eat in order to lose a pound a week? How often will you need to work out to get significantly fitter? How many more cold calls do you need to be making this week if you are planning on doubling your commissions over the month? It can feel very rewarding to achieve incremental improvements, even if you are still a long way off from your big reward. The biggest problem with having a big dream that you haven't chunked down into manageable steps, is that it can tend to appear overwhelming and unachievable.

Small, tangible steps that lead to mid-range milestones will significantly improve your likelihood of remaining focused long enough to realize your dreams. Setting up incremental markers will provide many encouraging reminders that you are making progress, and keep you going when the end goal is still a long way off.

How will you know you are making the right kind of progress and not just feeling busy, doing stuff that won't get you what you want? Simple – make your goals as smart as your phone has become.

SMART GOALS ARE:

Specific

Measurable

Achievable

Relevant

Time-based

If you follow that strategy, all your goals will be: attached to a deadline; related to your purpose; possible to accomplish; able to be quantified; and very, very clear. Having clear sight of your target will increase your likeliness of hitting it. You'll need to invest a little time into figuring out how to recognize when you've reached your targets, and how much time it will take. It's also wise to consider what obstacles might be standing in their way and then come up with a few strategies for getting around them.

Going over obstacles, digging underneath them, blowing them up and dissolving them should not be ruled out. Even if that sentence doesn't make logical sense to you, be open to thinking outside the box and you might realize something traditional thinking was keeping from you. Do not get stuck in any habitual ways of thinking. Be creative if you are seeking novel solutions. Ponder the hurdles and wonder what would help you to keep moving. As long as you do not give up, you will arrive somewhere along the way.

Remember: one success generally motivates another success more often than missing the mark does. If you aim for manageable, measurable goals, you will avoid biting off more than you can chew. You will feel automatically encouraged to continue and avoid the demotivating force of failure. To get you thinking about the small steps that will lead you to your ideal outcome, I encourage you to start figuring it out now. To help you do that, here is a simple format you can follow to lay out your comprehensive goal strategy:

GOAL FOCUSING EXERCISE

1. In the following Goal Mapping Outline, begin by stating your big goal in a simple declarative sentence. For example: By 2020, I am awarded salesperson of the year. Or, by 2025 I own my own home outright.

2. Next, list all the midway milestones that would naturally lead you to succeed at reaching that big goal, like increasing your sales quota, doubling your prospect list, shedding five pounds, getting promoted to a more lucrative position at work or renovating your current home to increase its resale value. Be as specific as possible and remember to follow the rest of the SMART goal statement creation strategy.

3. Finally, make a list of all the activities that you can do in order to reach each of the milestones you've set for yourself. Each of these small achievable steps should also follow the SMART formula, even if many of them are tasks you will repeatedly work at each week. For example, you might need to eat five to ten fruits and vegetables every day in order to diminish your appetite for the junk food that would otherwise stop you from dropping a dress size or shrinking down your buddha belly.

You can use the following format to begin your action plan. You may need to enlarge it or spread it over several separate pages. Tailor this template to suit your needs. Keep in mind that things not fitting the format is <u>not</u> an excuse to give up. It's just a tiny challenge to overcome. Rise to the challenge and prove to yourself that you really, really are planning to do what it takes to succeed. Then fill in the details that you can follow. It's good to have clearly defined targets.

GOAL MAPPING OUTLINE - a.k.a. ACTION PLAN

BIG JUICY GOAL (Destination)

○	

MID-RANGE MILESTONES (Along the way)

○	
○	
○	
○	
○	

SMALL MANAGEABLE STEPS (Directly in front of you)

○	
○	
○	
○	
○	
○	
○	
○	
○	
○	
○	

If you have more than one big goal, you'll need to consider each goal separately on separate action plans. Once you've done that and you've laid out your plans on paper or into a spreadsheet, decide for yourself which goal you are going to get started on first. It is recommended that you do not try to focus on more than one big goal at a time.

It is better to give your full attention to just a single goal to get started, and to give the new behaviours at least a month to form into habits. Better still is giving them eight or even twelve weeks to blossom before you plant more, especially if the new ones are big. Too many people unknowingly sabotage themselves by having a habit of thinking they can do it faster. Don't be one of them but be open to being pleasantly surprised if it does happen faster for you. Take your time in attending to them until they've taken root and can survive without your conscious care.

You might need to regularly update some of the specific weekly tasks, that once accomplished, will no longer need repeating. Or, they may be the kind of activities that you will perform over and over again, leading you closer and closer to your mid-range targets. Don't be put off if your goals need revisiting. Simply make revisiting your goals one of the regularly specified tasks on your list of habits to routinely nurture. What gets tracked tends to get done—but having too many planned tasks in the air at once might get overwhelming. For that reason, you may benefit from tackling each of the mid-range goals one at a time.

YOU CAN'T DO IT ALL AT ONCE

It's been proven that conscious multitasking is basically a myth, since the average human mind can only focus effectively on one thing at a time. Even if we are capable of spinning seven plates, we can only be spinning one of them at a time, in any given moment. When you were in school, you were able to handle several subjects a day and run through the entire gamut of your educational curriculum every single week. Juggling many different tasks, compartmentalized into different hourly blocks, is not the same as trying to study all your subjects at the same time. We can only focus on one thing at a time, but time can be divided much more effectively than our concentration could ever be.

Set time aside for reviewing your daily goals every day, in addition to achieving the items on your list. Whilst writing this book, I was also seeing clients, working on promotional material for my latest keynote, brainstorming novel ideas for upgrading my goal acing seminar, renewing my psychotherapy license, paying my bills, connecting with friends, taking my dog to the vets and reading research articles. Of course, I also continued my habits of hygiene and I even ate three meals a day and drank copious cups of Earl Grey tea.

Like plate spinning, I focused on each activity exclusively while I was doing it, especially the tea drinking. But then I swiftly turned my attention to the next task on my daily task list once the previous task was completed (or I needed a break). I would not have liked to have spent months on end focused solely on mathematics every hour of the day at school. I liked to turn my attention to English or art on occasion, intuitively understanding that "a change is as good as a rest." So, I did not always succeed with accomplishing every task on the list before switching my attention to something else, but when I did complete a tricky new task, I made sure to reward myself for being such a good boy and deserving an "A."(I also gave my poor pup a treat or two for being such a good girl at the vets.)

With that goal mapping exercise under your belt, you'll be much clearer about what you want to achieve and why. Clearly, making the list of activities you need to engage in, and setting the milestones is not your end goal. It's just a start, but it is a great start, and lightyears from what lazy no-hopers have accomplished in pursuit of their dreams. Without this kind of clarity, how would you be able to really get going on your goal? You could easily burn through all your fuel and get nowhere by driving hard in the wrong direction. But with the destination determined, you can now begin your journey, safe in the knowledge that the harder you go at it, the sooner you'll arrive at your destination.

Of course, just like a Formula One race car driver, it pays to know the course off by heart, inside and out. You might not be driving at a dangerous speed on the road to where you are going, but having the route programmed into your GPS means you won't have to fuss about with maps that slow you down and cause you to take your eyes off the road. Getting your goals, milestones and sequential steps burned into your brain, will make you far more effective in navigating your way there. You won't be caught off guard, and you'll definitely know what to say when someone asks you.

ACE YOUR GOALS

In the following chapters, we are going to look at the different routes you can easily take to teach your brain what you want it to make second nature for you. It pays to work with reality, so hoping they sink in, is not going to be as effective as using a few simple psychological strategies to encourage them into your neurology. Ignoring any sixth sense you may have, your sense of balance, sense of self and sense of right and wrong, you've only got five recognized senses that inform you about you and the world around you.

Experiencing anything in the sensory realms of touch, sight, sound, smell and taste, are the only five ways that you know you are not dead. They are not evidence that you are awake however, since your dreaming mind can play tricks on you and it can vividly imagine (aka hallucinate) in every one of those five senses. Regardless, awake or asleep, your senses are the only avenues to bringing anything into your experience and the only pathways to programming your own brain.

In the following three chapters, you are going to see how you can make efficient use of the primary pathways to programming goals into your mind. Namely auditory, kinaesthetic and visual (aka sounds/words, sensations/feelings and sights/images). You'll gain an understanding of how you can utilize them all in a regime of affirming, conditioning and envisioning, to internalize your goal destination and form positive habits that will get you there. What could be better than acing a desirable goal?

Well, I'm going to show you exactly how you can **ACE** your goal and achieve it with ease....by **A**ffirming, **C**onditioning and **E**nvisioning your action plan into your subconscious mind where it can influence you at all times, outside of your awareness, with no conscious effort required. But before I do that, here's a reminder of some of what we've covered in this chapter:

CHAPTER 4 SUMMARY

AKA:

WHAT YOU'VE LEARNED BY READING THIS CHAPTER

1. Focus all your attention on a clear target, and do not get fixated on or distracted by anything else.

2. Don't aim for something you aren't prepared to hit.

3. Make sure you choose a goal that you find compelling enough to commit to.

4. Chunk your goal down into smaller achievable pieces.

5. Set yourself up for small success after small success along the way.

DAVID FAIRWEATHER

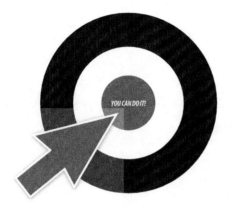

CHAPTER 5

AFFIRMING YOUR GOALS

AKA

REMINDING YOURSELF
WHAT YOU'LL DO AND WHY

In principle, there is not a single person on this planet that cannot ride to the top of a skyscraper in an enclosed elevator. There are however, a great number of people who believe they can't. Whether you believe you can or believe you can't, what you tell yourself has an impact. "I can do it" is just as powerful as "I can't do it". The power that either phrase elicits propels us in opposite directions. Conflicting messages promote uncertainty and lock us in indecision, or an auditory tug of war.

Want to earn more tips waiting tables, more commissions selling cars, or really get your money's worth out of being coached? Set it as an intention, by telling yourself that you will listen to your next client or your current coach immediately before your next interaction with them. Remind yourself to pay attention to them – to really, deeply listen, and with the intention set, it's much likelier to happen than if you merely left it to chance. Good habits tend to be developed on purpose.

We all entertain voices in our heads and our habit is to obey the most compelling voice, whether it's the voice of reason or an unreasonable, unsettling voice of fear. "I <u>can</u> do this", "Who am I kidding?! THIS IS NOT POSSIBLE FOR ME..." Ultimately, the most powerful voice with the strongest pull wins. Your self-talk massively impacts the outcome of any endeavour. It even impacts you more than encouraging or damning words from outside sources. Think about it. Would you really take onboard the encouraging words of another if you kept telling yourself that they just weren't true? Doubt and disbelief are not conducive to confidence and commitment, unless you want to be confident that you are committing to failure.

Since your expectation greatly governs the level of determination you experience, I firmly suggest telling yourself that whatever you are hoping to achieve is possible. John Henry Ford, the visionary responsible for crank-starting the entire automotive industry, was famous for saying "Whether you think you can or you think you can't, you're right". Doubt must be eradicated if you want a fair chance at succeeding at anything. I wish I had the conviction I enjoy today when my doctor was entrancing me with her magic spell of, "You will always have this pain!". But I won't punish myself for not knowing back then what I understand to be so important now.

GOING UP?

Confident inner dialogue is a major auditory aid to success. If you don't know what to tell yourself, you'll suffer from missed opportunities to boost your morale and motivate yourself to focus on the positive when doubt tries to creep into your mind. Think of it like a personal elevator pitch. An elevator pitch is what you'd tell Richard Branson about your business if you found yourself on a 30-second journey with him, trapped in a small metal room that rapidly takes the hard work out of slowly climbing your way to the top. If you don't know what you'd say given that golden opportunity to pique his interest and get his meeting planner's number, then you'll probably sound a lot less inspiring as you struggle to figure it out on the spot. You cannot make a second first impression with someone else, but you can always revamp and reinvent the ideas you impress upon yourself.

Your personal elevator pitch should effortlessly move you to feel confident. That comes from knowing exactly what you will say to yourself when you need to feel more motivation. Do not put yourself on the spot when it comes time to defend yourself against doubt, or to convince yourself that you are capable. It's one thing to dismiss doubt, but when you empty your mind of a thought, your momentarily vacuous head is immediately going to fill up again with something.

AUDITORY EXERCISE #1

THINKING FORK

1. Think nothing but the word "Fork, fork, fork" for 30 seconds.

2. After 30 forkful seconds, try not to think the word "fork", and instead, try to think absolutely nothing.

3. Notice what happens in the 30 seconds that follow your "forky" thoughts.

So, what did happen? Did you do it or aren't you taking this book seriously? Did you manage to think absolutely nothing, or did some words pop into your mind? Were they random words or related to fork, like knife, spoon, table or plate? Maybe you had some negative thoughts about the exercise, or possibly you had the realization that it's impossible to think about nothing?

When I teach mindfulness and meditation methods, I'm frequently reminded that there is a false belief permeating our understanding of a meditative mindset. The misunderstanding many people fall under the spell of is that meditating masterfully means "thinking no thoughts". Your mind is like a dripping tap. Thoughts will keep plopping into your mind like water drops falling into the sink from a leaky faucet. The only way to stop all thoughts entirely would involve removing your brain from your skull, and that would be a dumb idea to entertain. Developing your ability to tighten control over the rate of thought-drips so that you can enjoy moments of silent relief in between them, is a more realistic expectation to have.

DUMP THE BAD AND KEEP THE GOOD

Redirecting negative thoughts straight down the drain while you purposefully catch positive ones that can accumulate in your mind, is something you can easily learn to do. If you find yourself thinking "I can't do this", all you have to do is stop thinking that thought the moment you become aware of it, and immediately replace the thought with "I can do this." It's like the negative words can be sucked out of your awareness and the vacuum left in your head can be filled with positivity-generating thoughts that leave no room for the doubts to return. Sure, they might try to play in your head again, but as long as you don't give up draining them away and bathing in positive words, you'll be brainwashing yourself in the best possible sense.

To help you experience this, try the following exercise:

AUDITORY EXERCISE #2

COUNTING TO FOUR

1. Decide now that in a moment you'll set a timer for two full minutes and close your eyes until the timer tells you to open them.

2. With your eyes closed, begin counting slowly from 1 to 4 and only think the numbers 1, 2, 3 and 4. I'd tell you to count 1 elephant, 2 elephants, etc., only I don't want you thinking about elephants!

3. Should anything other than the numbers enter your mind, even the realization that two minutes is almost over, simply go back to counting, beginning every time at 1.

4. If you do get to 4, simply begin again at 1. But if anything else, even the thought: "I'm doing great at this" enters your mind on any level, immediately disengage from that thought and go straight back to 1.

Instructions clear in your mind? All you are going to do is entertain four numbers in your head and immediately dump any other words or thoughts that attempt to steal your attention and replace them with the single thought of "1, 2, 3, 4".

Ok, we'll continue from here, now go.

Welcome back! Hopefully, you didn't get to 4. If you did, it's more likely that you tricked yourself into believing you did, rather than discovering that you have immense power over your own thinking. It could happen, but I doubt it. You might have chosen to ignore some random, spontaneous thoughts, but if you didn't simultaneously return to 1, you have misinterpreted the exercise I intended to have you follow. There are always at least two aspects to any communication: The intention behind the transmitter and the interpretation of the receiver. One of the realizations I hoped you'd arrive at via that quick exercise, was a greater awareness of the density of thought traffic racing through your gridlocked mind.

YOU CAN'T STOP THINKING

The average adult human being has somewhere between 60,000 and 70,000 thoughts a day, depending on whose research you read. That is a LOT of thoughts! It would boil down to about 48 thoughts a minute if you were awake for 24 hours straight. Calculating sleep into the equation, that is at least one thought every single second that you are awake. Turning the dripping tap off is pretty much impossible, but with a greater degree of self-mastery, you can learn to entertain fewer thoughts.

Entertaining productive thoughts and letting negative thoughts go is a skill anyone can improve at. Confident people dismiss fleeting worries so well that they are often unaware that they do it. It has become second nature to them like playing the piano is to a seasoned pianist. Anxious and pessimistic people aren't flawed or broken, they are just used to engaging with the worst aspects of their imagination. They might not have learned what confident optimists do in their minds to defuse demotivating ideas.

In the cognitive reprogramming discipline of NLP (Neuro-Linguistic Programming) a technique known as the "Auditory Swish" is an excellent method taught to clients who are bothered by unwelcome thoughts. It is not difficult to do and takes seconds to learn. Based on the principle that you cannot have no thoughts, clients are conditioned to replace problematic thoughts with specific self-affirming thoughts repeatedly until its almost impossible to think the negative thought without the positive thought tagging along and eventually replacing it entirely. It's a technique best done rapidly, hence the "swish", however it could just as easily have been named the "auditory whoosh!"

The positive, self-affirming statements we are going to generate in this chapter will make perfect replacements for any demotivating thoughts that pop into your mind. Rather than engaging with negative thoughts or entertaining them, in the same way that you replaced your thoughts for the numbers 1 through 4, you will simply exchange your positive affirmations for them. To illustrate: if you found yourself thinking "I'm never going to be able to play the piano", you'd simply cut off that line of reasoning and declare confidently instead: "I can make improvements in anything I continue to practice".

I'm not looking for outlandish optimism here, just something more realistic and a lot less dismissive of your potential. "I can't do it" can easily change to "I might just be able to do it", or even "I can do anything I set my mind to". "I'm so stupid" can change to "Everyone makes mistakes", and "It's impossible" is possible to exchange with "I'm going to figure this out". Or at least, "I'll find a way to figure it out somehow."

There are always at least two ways to look at things – positively and negatively. Neither way is accurate or absolute. Both opinions are a subjective assessment. You can learn to be optimistic about your ability to improve in whatever way you want, just so long as you don't want to violate the laws of physics or nature. You can't get taller if you are in your thirties. You cannot grow bigger breasts either. You could get lifts or implants though, so maybe think outside the box a little if you really want something that isn't immediately understood as possible.

MOVED BY MERE WORDS

The words you entertain in your own mind have immense power over you. What use would cheerleaders be if the teams they cheered on did not buy into their optimism? I could tell you that your aspirations are attainable, but if you disagree, you win. (Remember John Henry Ford?) Your stream of consciousness, experienced as an auditory hallucination of a voice speaking a language in your head, impresses ideas into your neurology. This is where the term Neuro-Linguistic Programming originates. Cheerleaders don't make up their message on the spot. They've already got it planned and ready to motivate their team at the moment they need to hear it.

Ideas turn into action because ideas stimulate emotion and emotion causes motion. "Ideomotor activity" is the term used for ideas translated into motor-movement. Whenever you've found yourself gripping the arm of a chair or your partner during a riveting thriller, the idea of tension communicated by the director has caused your hand to grab out subconsciously. You could even tell yourself not to do it again, and then find your nails digging into flesh or fabric just moments later. Horror films can make you jump or trigger goosebumps. Before they were films, they were words in a screenplay. Words can move someone to tears, or cause them to tremble uncontrollably, but only when the recipient is aware of them and is filling their mind or dominating their thoughts with them.

Well, that last statement isn't strictly true. The discipline of cognitive behavioural therapy (aka CBT), is founded on the robustly proven theory that we are profoundly impacted by thoughts we are not even consciously aware of. Influenced by the work of 20th century psychologists: Albert Ellis and Aaron Beck, CBT is a modality of psychotherapy aimed at bringing subconscious, "automatic thoughts" into conscious awareness, where they can be evaluated and disarmed by reason. Statistically, CBT is the preferred form of psychotherapy prescribed by doctors in North America for depression and anxiety.

Not quite the same thing as purposefully thinking positively motivating thoughts to influence yourself, CBT is still operating on the principle that our thoughts influence our feelings and influence our behaviour. The following exercise, when done correctly, will leave you with no doubts about that.

THOUGHTS INTO MOTION

1. You do not have to buy a pendulum for this simple demonstration of how the power of words can affect your body. But if you have one, please use it for this exercise. If you don't have one, simply find a necklace with a heavy pendant on it or tie a nut or a few washers onto the end of a length of string or thread.

2. With the weight hanging about 6"-8" from your thumb and fingers of the hand holding the other end, place your elbow on the arm of a chair and stare at the weighted end.

3. Repeat the words "Left – Right" over and over in your mind and continue to stare at the pendulum.

4. Simply "want" the pendulum to respond to your verbal coaxing and do not resist any movement that occurs.

5. Definitely do not fight the response, and whatever you do, do not tell yourself that it is a ghost moving it! (That might just trigger gooseflesh!)

6. After you see the efforts of your verbal commands moving the pendulum, try the words: "Back and forth" followed a little later by "Round and round"

What you will find is that without your conscious manipulation, the pendulum does indeed respond to your thoughts. It's as if someone else were moving it, but I assure you that it was no spectre. Ideomotor movements in the form of micromuscular activity was the culprit. Tiny muscular movements outside of your conscious perception. Not unlike the kind of subconscious activity that moves you closer towards people you are attracted to when sitting next to them, engaged in a compelling conversation.

If you found yourself nodding in agreement with that last statement, your unintentional head nod was simply another form of ideomotor movement. It's very difficult to pretend you are attracted to someone that repulses you, and it's hard to feign agreement with something you find objectionable. Your body will give you away to anyone well versed in the language of the body. When I'm coaching anyone, I'm always paying attention to signs, that what they are telling me is congruent with what they believe at a deep level.

DO YOU REALLY MEAN WHAT YOU SAY?

Congruence between what you feel and what you say is vital if you are going to communicate honestly, in both body language and verbal language. Although it's been shown that suppressing negative thoughts isn't helpful, acknowledging them and establishing more reasonable alternative thoughts, is useful. For that reason, I highly recommend believable affirmations that shift you from negativity without triggering absolute disbelief. If you want to convince yourself that something difficult is possible, "I might be able to do this" is better than "I could never do it". Thinking, "I can do it with my hands tied behind my back" might trigger your B.S. alarm! (B.S. is a technical term meaning bogus statement, if you believe that.)

It won't take that much persistence to go from thinking, "I cannot play the piano" to "I can play a few notes". But to become fluent in a new skill like juggling chainsaws or speaking French, might require time to accomplish. If you give up trying, your failure is secured. But keep at it, and you might just surprise yourself!

When I first arrived in Canada, I was fascinated by the people I met that could speak both French and English. It seemed that they had mastered something incomprehensible to me at the time. But learning a new language is something so rudimentary that even small children can do it (and they do!). Adults often tell themselves that they could never learn a new language. If they believe that, they'll probably never even try.

A great, French speaking man from the 1800s that you might not have heard of is Émile Coué. You've almost certainly heard his famous saying: "Every day, in every way, I am getting better and better". There are a few slightly different translations of that phrase, but one of the most famous interpretations of it was by Lennon and McCartney in the Beatles song "Getting Better".

YOU DON'T HAVE TO BE SICK TO GET BETTER

Coué's work wasn't accepted by the mainstream public at the time, but much of it has recently been proven to be effective by modern science. It's really not that different from CBT, since both modalities are focused on helping sick people feel better. You do not have to be sick to get better. With the right mindset, you can make improvements at almost anything. I tend to rationalize that if cheerleaders can change the behaviour of world class athletes, simply by offering them positive suggestions, everyone can use good self-suggestions to make improvements in their own responsive actions. In essence, we can all improve by adopting the right mindset, and our own words are one of the best routes to doing that.

Negative internal dialogue and self-deprecating inner chatter are both great avenues to feeling bad about yourself and getting demotivated. But positive self-talk and self-affirming statements are a wonderful way to lift your own spirits and elevate your expectations about what is possible for you to achieve. Repeat a few choice phrases enough times and they'll tend to become as automatic as well rehearsed cheers. These automatic thoughts are simply habits of thinking that have formed strong neurological pathways in our brains and have become as effortless as driving. CBT "pokes around in your mind" and helps you to become aware of them. Good or bad, what we say to ourselves has impact. Anyone who argues with that truth, has a strong voice negating reality in their head.

The words of others are also powerful. Being asked, "You don't want frozen fries and watered down drinking syrup with that nostril and eyelid patty right now, do you?" would glean less positive results in a burger joint than "Would you like to take advantage of our super-combo money-saver today?". "Don't forget not to be late again tomorrow, moron," wouldn't be as effective a motivator as: "Remember to be on time or early tomorrow, please." Whether you are biased negatively or positively, it is going to influence how you feel and in turn how you respond.

THE POWER OF I AM

Words have power. Some of the most powerful words we use tend to immediately follow the words: "I am...".

- "I am bad at math," tends to make attempting trigonometry feel pointless.

- By contrast, "I am going to figure this out," would encourage far more hope.

- "I am never going to lose weight," would not be as useful as:

- "I am definitely getting into that dress by my birthday."

- "I am relaxed and calm, and I can cope," are certainly better things to tell yourself when you need to keep your cool than:

- "This is going to go so badly and hurt so much!"

Talking to yourself in the mirror, takes the power of affirmation up a notch. It might be the act of saying it out loud rather than merely thinking it that kicks your self-talk into another gear, but the more likely reason it works is that the act of looking yourself in the eye while speaking to yourself has a powerful psychological effect. Psychologist Thomas Harris and his Transactional Analysis colleagues in the 1960's called this technique "Mirror Work." Research on mirror work suggests that it can take hundreds of repetitions before the self-statements become fully-believed, automatic thoughts. That might seem like a lot of work, but the good news is that it might only take a few hundred repetitions before your feelings, behaviour and ultimately your life is changed by them!

I have a few ways to supercharge mirror work that I teach in seminars and to my private coaching clients, but any way you work at getting a message through to your yourself in the mirror is going to lead to some improvement. You might be telling yourself that it is not worth trying, but if you are influenced by that thought, then you'll see the sense of speaking to yourself in order to influence your behaviour. If you feel silly pretending you can do something that you don't yet believe you can do, rest assured that "making believe" long enough to make an actual belief, isn't risking very much embarrassment at all.

I'm not telling you to prematurely announce your positive or neutralizing new thought to anyone. But if you do announce your intentions to accomplish something, science says you'll be far likelier to achieve it than if you keep your proclamation to yourself. Telling the world, or at least a friend, a coach, or an accountability partner, is a great way to motivate yourself. We humans do not like being wrong, since we find it threatening. Sometimes you need the threat of failure barking behind you to keep you forging forward. Don't tell anyone, and it's far easier to talk yourself out of following through on your unpublicized claims.

Your daily activities should support your mid-range targets, which should in turn assist in accomplishing your big juicy dream. If you are anticipating any obstacles or hurdles that will make overcoming any of the simple steps more challenging, spend a little time coming up with practical solutions and encouraging words that will help keep you from giving up and rationalizing why it cannot be done. You may have to invest more than a few minutes at this stage, but having a solution-focused plan in your back pocket will save you time, tension and tears later. Your SMART goals, hurdle-overcoming plans and the positive, reinforcing messages you make from them, will give you tangible tools that you can easily use in order to stay motivated to succeed. Then all you need to do is make a habit of putting them to work.

AUDITORY EXERCISE #4

BUILDING AFFIRMATIONS

1. To get started on structuring your own success-affirming thoughts that you want to program into your own head, simply take the goals you put to paper in the last chapter and turn them into simple declarative statements that keep the point in mind.

2. The big goal might be far off, but keep any concrete steps in the present tense and arrange them in a: BECAUSE-ACHIEVE / BECAUSE-DO format.

    For example: "Because I'd love to drive around in a sexy red convertible this year, I am doubling my commissions this month, because I make twenty cold calls every day of the work-week".

    (You can also think of that as an: "I desire x so I do y by doing z every day" affirmation if those words speak to your mindset more.)

Over the years I've suggested to many people that they record their goals on tape. (More recently, I recommend creating a Self-Propelling Sound-File™ on their smartphone.) It's been fascinating just how many of them doubted that it would work before they even tried it. That takes judging a book by its cover to another level! When I inquired why, many of them told me that they doubted that they'd believe all the things they'd tell themselves. Even lies we tell ourselves can become our truths eventually.

If you can access the kind of neurological chemistry that you experience whenever you tell yourself something that you *do* believe, I'd definitely recommend bringing your new affirmations into that mindset, or modifying the way that you talk to yourself, until it triggers the same kind of chemical cascade. Logic aside, what is it about the way you say believable things that makes them feel different? Are they louder or clearer? Does the tone of your voice alter the way you feel about what you hear yourself saying? Do you breathe differently or hold your posture another way? If you need help with those subtleties, finding an experienced NLP practitioner to work with might be a good option to tell yourself to pursue.

Maybe you just need to hear them more often until they feel familiar? Émile Coué's advice was to repeat them to yourself twenty times each night as you fall asleep and twenty times each morning as soon as you awaken. He recommended using a piece of string with twenty knots on it, so that you don't have the distraction of having to keep count in your head.

Depending on how quickly you fall asleep, and whether you feel like doing it every night and every morning, that sage advice might work well for you. If it doesn't, or the idea doesn't appeal to you, let's look at some other options for getting your words to work for you in the following chapters. Hopefully, the principles we've covered in this chapter give you some clarity around the significance of your own internal dialogue. Let's review:

CHAPTER 5 SUMMARY

AKA:

WHAT YOU'VE LEARNED BY READING THIS CHAPTER

1. We all have doubts, but we don't all dwell on them.

2. Being focused is a nurtured habit, regardless of the nature of our focus.

3. The words you entertain inside your head influence you more than those that come from outside.

4. Keeping in mind the reasons why you committed to do things will make it more likely that you'll do them.

5. Reminding yourself of your focus often, is a great aid to committing it to memory and motivating yourself.

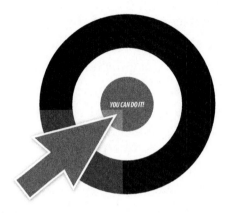

CHAPTER 6

CONDITIONING PURPOSEFUL HABITS

AKA

MAKING SUCCESSFUL HABITS ON PURPOSE

It's often been said, in varying ways, that: "Once is an accident, twice is a coincidence and three times is a habit". If you have established the daily activities you need to focus on, and you've figured out whatever words encourage you to get them accomplished, all you must do now is develop the habit of doing them. It's one thing having great affirmations in your motivational action plan, but if you never use them, don't look at them, or hardly hear them, they aren't really going to help you overcome your old habits and become the best possible you any time soon.

117

Not taking the time to work out your own mind-priming statements is one tactic to keeping things the way they are. Is that what you would like? Working them out and then not putting them to work "yet", is another level entirely, of resisting reaching for your dreams. You've got to put your words to work if you are going to turn a big dream into reality.

Recording them so that you can passively listen to them and subliminally absorb them, is a great way to get them burned painlessly into your brain. We'll look at ways to do that effectively in a later chapter, but first let's look at some ways of hammering them home that doesn't rely on electricity or any other form of external power.

THE POWER WITHIN

Your first new habit needs to be: looking at what really needs doing and then telling yourself whatever you need to hear, to see that you get it done.

I'm not sure how good you are with accomplishing new or repeatedly scheduled tasks, but if you have a habit of forgetting to implement things, I'm going to need you to become more accountable for your actions (or inaction). I want you to wonder for a while, what small but immediate penalty, deterrent or consequence you feel would be appropriate to impose upon yourself, should you forget to utilize the resourceful statements that you've invested your time into crafting?

You may need to begin changing your life by first holding yourself accountable for using your life-changing affirmations. New activities are always somewhat more awkward and cumbersome than familiar habits. Whenever you have to drive to a new location, it always feels like a longer journey than repeated trips to familiar destinations. When you are first learning a new language, it can be harder and take significantly longer to find the words that express what you want to communicate in that new language, than your native tongue. After a period of persistent efforts, eventually it will become second nature, thanks again to Hebb's law.

I've used this theory in working with therapy clients in the past that were very negative towards themselves or life in general. Chronic pessimism isn't that different from chronic English or chronic French. Each of them is a way of thinking and expressing oneself. A diligent student of French will one day find themselves spontaneously thinking in French. Committed students of optimism trying to break the habit of spontaneous negative thoughts will also succeed, eventually. We all have the capacity to think positively about things. Some people may just need to develop the habit.

KEEP IT UP

If you could develop a routine of giving yourself a powerful pep talk every single day, do you think you'd feel more motivated to act on your daily goals, or less? Obviously, it won't be less, unless you've been unrealistic or over-enthusiastic in your expectations. Well, science says that it generally takes about 21 days to make or break a habit, so all you'll need to commit to, is about three weeks to a month of conscious effort before you'll find yourself subconsciously motivated to continue with your new habit, which will by then will feel familiar.

Making and breaking habits can literally be considered as programming or reprogramming muscle memories in your body and the neurological pathways in your brain. Everyone's body and brain differ somewhat, and we can all perceive different habits as presenting different levels of threat, reward, pain and discomfort. The suggested 21 days is an arbitrary number, in the same way that 7.5 hours of sleep a night and 2000 calories a day are generally recommended for all adults regardless of their specific age, weight, height, occupation and lifestyle. You might need to go longer than 21 days, or you might get the habit programmed in more quickly.

Having made the commitment to make using your life-changing affirmations a part of your daily activities can feel really rewarding. Forgetting to engage with them and missing out on the motivation they'd naturally mobilize could feel somewhat of a punishment. Something more rewarding, is an actual reward and something more punishing is an actual punishment. Think about what little treat, or personal pleasure would feel motivating to get for your self-programming activities. While you ponder that, maybe you've already figured out what forfeit you feel would fit the crime of letting yourself be lazy or absent minded? Are you going to wash the dishes by hand tonight? Miss your favourite TV show, or drink water instead of wine with your meal? Or drive the side streets home after work instead of taking the fast route? The punishment doesn't have to be harsh. Just a deterrent to the act of dismissing your goal-seeking behaviours and not taking them seriously.

Taking steps towards failure should be punishing enough, but just in case it isn't, you might need to feel some unpleasantness for it to be effective. Not doing what you should be doing, should probably come with a price tag *now* rather than a much bigger disappointment later, don't you agree? Would you use your credit card less often, if every time you used it you had to mail a cheque for $10 to an organization you despise (like a dogmeat farm or something else repellent)? What if the amount of the cheque doubled with every payment you mailed to them?

Great new positive habits are naturally rewarding. But their initial steps may not seem so at first. Try to develop the habit of juggling chainsaws, and more than likely the pain of failure would abruptly end all future attempts (well, that and losing a hand or two!). Nikolai Rimsky-Korsakov's "Flight of the Bumblebee" is not recommended as a first composition to master if you have no previous piano skills. Taking on a big challenge without building yourself up will not allow you to feel regular doses of encouraging competence.

Science shows us that humans learn from rewarding desirable behaviour more than punishments. Small, incremental, rewarding steps are the key to building a new sustainable habit. Repeating what is enjoyable fast-tracks the new learning into your long-term cognitive and muscular memory banks. If you do not enjoy what you are doing, you will be more likely to subconsciously avoid the behaviour rather than integrate it effectively into your repertoire of soft skills. Repetitive punishments can easily attach their feeling state to the pursuit of your goals, and we wouldn't want that. As science shows, delayed punishments are ineffective at correcting behaviours and mindsets. They can be useful, however, in creating the desire to avoid the consequences that they offer.

SMART PHONE, STUPID ME

Thanks to my growing reliance on a smart phone, there are very few phone numbers that I have memorized in my mind these days. Most of them I've only entered once into my mobile device. My smart phone can do all my remembering for me and I don't have to do it. It's not really that my smart phone has made me stupid, but it has taken away the necessity to commit new phone numbers to memory. Unused neurological paths tend to fade. That's a good thing when I'm working to help people change bad habits, but when it comes to life skills, you might want to trigger the circuits from time to time so they don't get rusty, forgotten, diminished or rendered inexistent.

Should I ever deem it necessary to learn a new phone number, all I'd need to do is *want* to commit it to memory and program it into my neurology using repetition (remember Hebb's law?). At first, the new seven-digit sequence would be held loosely in my working memory, but over time, and with continued repetition, I'd know that number "by heart." Once it starts to enter my mind, all the connected numbers would come along for the ride like "John Lennon" brings to mind "the Beatles" and "Yoko Ono" – and possibly the song "Imagine." What "fires" together, truly does "wire" together!"

With that new number successfully ingrained into my entrained brain, simply imagining the person I wanted to call, and wondering what their new number is would bring their number to mind with no thinking required. If I did think hard about it, it wouldn't really help me. Stress and pressured thinking doesn't help, but relaxing and opening my mind to wonder what the number is, would be far more likely to aid me in realizing the valuable information I needed access to.

We really do not need to think about anything deeply conditioned into our neurology. Your dog doesn't have to think about what to do with dog food. If you do own a dog, you've probably noticed that your dog begins going wild at the sight of an unopened can of dog food, and gets nuts by the time your can opener is making its slicing sound though the top of the can? Almost everyone has heard of Pavlov's dogs, but in case you are amongst the 20% of the population that has not, Russian physiologist Ivan Pavlov discovered something very important at the end of the 19th century about the process of reflexive conditioning.

Pavlov was researching digestion and the role of salivation in canines by collecting saliva from the dogs at mealtimes. Each day a bell would be rung as the dogs were fed. One day, the bell was accidentally rung without presenting the dogs with any food because someone forgot to prepare the dog's dinner. Regardless of the absence of their meal, the dogs salivated anyway. They'd become conditioned to the sound of the bell being associated with food, and the bell now had the power to make the dogs dribble! They didn't have to think about it, it happened automatically. His accidental discovery has formed the bedrock in our understanding of the psychology of subconscious (aka unconscious) associative conditioning and habit formation.

"HIS MASTER'S BELL"

Some things make us feel good, and anything that reminds us of them will also trigger some measure of good feelings and related behaviour. The dogs were anticipating the flavour of food and the feeling of gustatory satiation that food delivers to them. Salivation is a natural reflexive response to the idea of eating, but salivating because a bell rings does not make any logical sense. The bell was a reminder of feeding time and the idea of food became a conditioned association. The repeated reward of food, that naturally triggers salivation, paired with the otherwise unrelated stimulus of a bell, lead to an unconscious link being formed between the bell and the salivation response.

Advertisers use this knowledge to their advantage when they place their products next to naturally stimulating visual cues like bikini clad models, hunky actors and well-liked celebrities. Our natural responses to ideas triggered by sexy stars and motivating personalities can very easily become neurologically paired with products placed in their proximity. It can also work the other way too. If you are offended by the scantily clad beauties bursting out of their itsy-bitsy, teenie-weenie, yellow polka dot bikinis, you'll probably feel somewhat antagonized whenever you see the related products sitting benignly on a shelf in the supermarket.

To give you a relatable experience, I'd like to expose you to the following simple demonstration of the power of your mind to be stimulated by ideas.

WARNING
DO NOT DO THE FOLLOWING EXERCISE IF YOU ARE ALLERGIC TO LEMONS

RESPONSE EXERCISE

THE JUICY LEMON

1. Please read though the instructions fully before clos-
    ing your eyes and imagining what I'm about to ask
    you to imagine. Alternately, log online and let me
    read the following to you.

2. Imagine for a few moments a firm, shiny, dimple-
    skinned lemon, sitting on a counter in front of you.

3. Pick it up in your mind and imagine feeling it's firm-
    ness and the weight of the lemon with your hand, as
    you hold it.

4. Imagine reaching out for a sharp knife and placing
    the lemon down on a cutting block.

5. Slice into the lemon with the knife, and watch the
    sour juice squirt from its flesh, as you cut the bitter
    lemon into two halves.

6. Smell the citrusy scent of lemon in your imagination
    and stare longingly at the soft, exposed lemon pulp
    in your mind's eye and remember what lemon juice is
    like to taste.

7. Bringing one half of the juicy lemon to your face,
    imagine squeezing its tart, sour juice onto your
    tongue, noticing whatever happens before you open
    your eyes and continue reading.

Ok – thanks for doing that. Hopefully you enjoyed the experience? If you gave it your all and were open to having the experience, you will have noticed the alteration of saliva that occurred in your mouth? **Newsflash:** There was no lemon, only the idea of a lemon. The words on this page that were entertained in your mind, acted like Pavlov's bell. If you've never seen a lemon and never tasted one before, it probably did not work on you, because your body would not previously have formed a reflexive response to lemons that could be triggered.

The reflexive response that you form to the idea of doing what you need to do to succeed in whatever you are hoping to accomplish, benefits greatly from memories of positive experiences. In the 1930's, a Harvard graduate student greatly influenced by Pavlov's research began studying the effect of rewards on the generation of behaviours. His name was Burrhus Frederic Skinner, better known in his day as psychologist and behaviourist; B.F. Skinner. Today, Google, Facebook and Twitter have been identified as utilizing "Skinnerian Marketing" to grow their cultures of widespread social networking to massive proportions.

Skinner was primarily concerned with the encouragement of specific behaviours rather than the triggering of subconscious responses. Skinner's research demonstrated how rewarding a pigeon for certain behaviours like flapping a wing or lifting a leg, will encourage the bird to do it again in the hopes of another reward. Essentially this is why dolphins are given fishy treats for jumping through hoops in their training. Skinner also studied the impacts of punishments. Using a device known as the "Skinner Box" that encourages invertebrates to stay on one side of the box by heating the other side whenever they wandered over the border, B.F. proved that behaviour can be conditioned with punishing heat.

Pavlov's work informed us how natural responses can become paired with unnatural cues like bells and whistles, and Skinner's research shows us how specific behaviours can be encouraged or discouraged with rewards and punishments. Regardless of the method utilized, all the responses elicited were essentially programmed into the neurological pathways residing in the brains of the test subjects. Building positive associations to rewarding responses, encourages behaviours to become automatic. Negative associations automatically discourage activities that aren't expected to have positive outcomes.

Back when I was developing carpal tunnel syndrome I'd learned that moving a computer mouse caused agonizing pain. It was the conditioned response that paired itself with manipulating a mouse that became "hard-wired" into my body and neurology. I'd accidentally trained myself to have chronic pain and to crave never having to move a mouse again. When I resigned from the high-tech position that required it, it felt much better than the pain.

HOLDING YOURSELF ACCOUNTABLE FOR YOUR SUCCESS

Science says conclusively that rewards for desirable behaviour are far more powerful than purposefully applied punishments for counter-productive actions. Even if the reward is simply a shot of dopamine delivered into your nervous system outside of your awareness, behaviours that lead you to feel good are more likely to be repeated, and behaviours that make you feel bad are more likely to be avoided.

Whenever dopamine is in your system, focusing becomes easier because the drug dopamine is pure ecstasy. Who could resist amplifying natural ecstasy? Things that do not excite us are more uninspiring than they are stimulating.

You might not find sticking to your diet exciting, but if you got rewarded every time you said "No" to chocolate and "Yes" to fruit, you'd be much more likely to feel good about eating an apple that wasn't dipped in candy. For a salesperson that desires stepping up to the next level in their organization, it might not feel fantastic *initially* to sacrifice fun time to make more cold calls. But, if you were to reward yourself in some way for your good behaviour, developing a good business habit of completing 10, 20 or more cold calls a day would be entirely possible to achieve relatively easily, regardless of how you feel about it today.

Without frequent rewards, motivation tends to get lost and we are more prone to distractions. Motivation is easy to diminish and even extinguish if the results of your behaviour are more unpleasant than they are pleasant. We definitely pay far more attention to what makes us feel good and we will certainly tend to avoid what we associate with making us feel bad. Like that donkey offered the carrot reward or the punishment of the stick to move, both reward and punishment have their place in motivating yourself to do what you need to do to hit your targets.

KNOW PAIN, KNOW GAIN?

New Year's exercisers fall prey to the pain of overreach every January. In the past, I've routinely told the following silly story to coaching clients and psychotherapy patients who tended to fail at achieving their physical fitness goals due to hitting the gym way too hard to ever be able to sustain. Before I share my story, I just want to make clear to any impressionable people reading this, that I'm not encouraging smoking in any way shape or form. My ridiculous metaphor is only intended to help you realize a simple truth about the risks of attempting too much too soon. With that said.....

If you were a non-smoker with the aspiration of becoming a two-pack-a-day smoker, the worst thing you could do is to smoke two packs of cigarettes on the very first day you decided to take up smoking. If you did, you'd more than likely feel very ill and associate that ill feeling with the idea of smoking. Becoming a two-pack-a-day smoker requires a simple strategy and some patience. You'd be well advised to just have a puff or two the first day. Nothing overwhelming and nothing that would create too strong a response to the toxic chemistry that would be administered into your lungs and distributed throughout your body and brain. Building up your tolerance incrementally by adding a few puffs each day would eventually condition you to be able to tolerate more and more of the pollution, as you habituate yourself to tolerating the smoky, smelly substance.

Smoking is quite nauseating at first puff, but anyone determined to get used to it, can. Exercise is really no different (apart from being good for you, not terrible). Do too much the first day, and tomorrow's pains will be a discouraging force in developing the healthy habit. If you could forget the old adage: "No pain, no gain" and focus instead on building the habit first before you add intensity, a few minutes enjoying the gym every day would rapidly accumulate into enjoying many minutes after a time.

Developing a sustainable habit is far more important than trying to achieve too much too soon, isn't it? Knowing that and believing it aren't the same thing, but if my outrageous smoking metaphor has helped a penny drop in your head, you'll understand that your binary brain will naturally gravitate to what feels good and avoid what leads to unpleasant consequences. Pleasurable or painful are the only options that your brain has for categorizing any experience. So, make sure that completing your concrete daily goals get rewarded in some experiential way, and that failing to do what you need to do has some unpleasant consequence associated to it. You really do benefit from rewarding yourself for a good job done well, and holding yourself accountable for any escaping your own commitments.

REWARDS AND PUNISHMENTS

1. Please make a list of small rewards and deterrents that would be possible for you to administer to yourself or remind yourself of while you work at conditioning productive purposeful habits into your brain and body. Please note: they should not be counterproductive to your goals. So please, no chocolate rewards if dropping excess weight is your desire.

2. Next, assign a rating of severity and arrange the list into a hierarchy of magnitude, so that you can easily discern the bigger rewards and more severe consequences from smaller, less compelling motivators. Big changes require bigger carrots and sharper sticks. Small changes, less so. The sticks in question are at least a clearer concept of the consequences and pains of failure.

3. When you have at least half a dozen or so rewards and a similar number of "discouragers", look over your short-term goals for the week. Decide which pleasurable rewards would motivate you to achieve the planned activities, and which unpleasant consequences would compel you to avoid cheating yourself out of accomplishing what you need to get done. Go with your gut about which punishments fit the crime of inaction. Don't think about it too much, as you might just start to convince yourself to ignore the advice, because at some level you'd already be planning to fail. If you are determined not to fail, the severity of the consequences shouldn't factor in, because you shouldn't be planning on making a habit out of failing.

To help you with that last exercise, please consider using the following format when completing your compelling lists of carrots and sticks: don't be too harsh when it comes to doling out what are effectively punishments, and don't be too lax, either. If you let yourself get away with murder, you've only got yourself to blame.

REWARDS & PUNISHMENTS

Enter your self-motivators and deterrents below along with their rating from 1-10

Level	Reward for Compliance	Level	Consequences of Avoidance
○		○	
○		○	
○		○	
○		○	
○		○	
○		○	
○		○	

If you have trouble thinking of enough rewards and you struggle to come up with compelling consequences, consider the following strategy:

CONDITIONING EXERCISE #2

A TOKEN REWARD SYSTEM

1. Think of a big gift, reward, present or acquisition that you'd love to earn and assign its value to a jar of pebbles.

2. Divide that value by the number of pebbles and re-move them from the jar.

3. Now simply reward behaviours that build the habits that get you to your goals, by adding a pebble to the jar each time you carry them out.

4. When the jar is full, go get that thing you promised to yourself, but whenever you engage in counterpro-ductive or achievement avoidant activities, you have to take a pebble out of the jar. Snakes and ladders isn't all up, and it isn't all equally as enjoyable.

DEVELOPING DISCIPLINE

Past a certain age, it's no longer fair to blame our parents, teachers or society for not protecting us from ourselves. It's one thing to want cigarettes to be hidden from our kids and not advertised on TV, but if you needed them hidden from yourself to avoid temptation you cannot resist, then you would be overly reliant on externally imposed restrictions. No-one else is going to make you do what you need to do but you. Restricting unhealthy things and counterproductive behaviours from ourselves, takes a measure of self-discipline that not everyone developed effectively in childhood (or in college).

Anyone who has ever been the driver on a road trip or a long journey, will have had the chance to feel dangerously tired behind the wheel at some point or other. You may have felt your eyelids growing heavy and experienced a growing tiredness that made the idea of letting them rest together for a few moments deliciously tempting. If you did give in and let that happen, you might be reading this book from your hospital bed. Hopefully you had the good sense to resist the urge!

Without some measure of self-discipline, we'd just mindlessly give into impulses, whenever they happened. We might even try justifying our behaviour as natural, and the denial of it as unnatural. I'm not denying that there are times when we feel tempted to give in to the idea of giving up, but if you never fight that feeling, your whole life would be at the mercy of your inner child or *id*. Children aren't great at delaying gratification, they often need help to develop that capacity from grown-ups.

Well, if you are grown up enough to be free of your parent's control, engaging in your own self-development to develop discipline could be the best investment in yourself that you ever make. As a child, you probably played a game called "Step on a crack, break your mother's back". No backs really got broken if you stepped between paving stones on your walk to school, but pretending that your mother would be paralyzed by your failure to concentrate on taking the right steps in the right way, very likely rendered fewer cracks being trodden upon between your house and the school gate.

Those best at playing video games effortlessly pretend that not getting their on-screen avatar killed, is vitally important even though no one really dies and there are no real consequences. I'm not suggesting imposing any real pain upon your poor mother. But I am suggesting that, without a looming concern connected to bad behaviour, you'll be less likely to make sure you do what you need to do, when you need to do it, like an adult.

I don't know about you, but I have a petulant teenager inside me that now and again wants me to break my own rules and do counterproductive things. Knowing that emotions are fleeting bursts of chemistry, I tend to make myself wait a little while before I make a decision about what to do. I try not to react on impulse. Prisons are literally full of people that do that!

No one would benefit from having their mother's back broken as an actual consequence of stepping on a crack in the pavement, but "step on a crack" certainly focuses those children who can effectively imagine undesirable consequences for failing to focus. Be careful with it though, there are enough anxious people that focus too much on big fearful consequences and effectively immobilize themselves in doing so. As Goldilocks is reported to have said, "Too much or not enough of anything is bad." (Or was that Buddha?).

WAIT FOR IT

For example, porridge isn't that bad for you, but if I get a pang of desire to eat something that isn't on my list of acceptable food options, I find that a short 15-minute wait before acting, nullifies a great many bad ideas from coming to fruition. Having a self-imposed consequence for breaking my own rule increases the likelihood that I will respect the rule. I can however, always break the rule if I'm willing to pay the self-imposed price. Rules without any consequences whatsoever, are as useless as teenagers without technology.

You probably don't let yourself drive drunk because of the police's rules about it, (and, of course, the dreadful thought of having another's blood on your hands). You can do whatever you feel like doing, or you can do what you need to do in order to reach your desired goal. There are always at least two ways of looking at everything, but sometimes you need to focus on the side of the argument that is in your long-term best interest. If you aren't a child anymore, you'll find that it really is possible to police yourself, if you really want to achieve something worth the effort.

What if you set yourself the immediate goal of making twelve completed sales calls today (or studying all day for an upcoming exam), but then feel like bailing after lunch and going to the movies instead? Would it really hurt to remind yourself what is so important about persevering and getting it done before you clock off for the day? Sure, taking an unscheduled break and letting yourself off the hook once in a while might be fun, but if you have a habit of impulsively giving up early and ditching your goal driving behaviours, it might be time to grow up a bit, Peter (or Penelope) Pan. You could rationalize that goals and plans are boring and spoil life's spontaneity. No-one is making you aim for more.

Your perspective is the only factor influencing you when it comes to achieving your goals and aspirations. It was the only factor causing you to avoid stepping on cracks on the way to school. If you view failing to succeed as a disabling injury to your career, self-esteem or ego, you'll probably do a better job than someone who can't see the harm in letting themselves get away with murdering their dreams.

Was that unnecessarily harsh? Well, it's tough to say, because there are at least two ways of looking at it, given that this *is* a three – dimensional universe. Just as you can have a habit of imagining you are bound to fail, you could develop the habit of seeing success as entirely possible. Let's take a look at how you see things now, as we delve deep into your subconscious self-image and where you see yourself in relation to everyone else, and your dreams. But first, a quick recap:

CHAPTER 6 SUMMARY

AKA:

WHAT YOU'VE LEARNED BY READING THIS CHAPTER

1. New, purposeful habits must be set intentionally.

2. If you let yourself fail to set the habits, you've only got yourself to blame.

3. Our likes and dislikes are learned habits that we tend to take for granted.

4. Rewards for good behaviour work better than punishments, but deterrents and consequences do have their place.

5. A token system of saving for a big reward, can also be utilized for imposing motivating consequences.

DAVID FAIRWEATHER

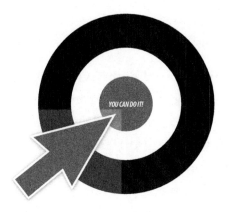

CHAPTER 7

ENVISIONING EXCELLENCE

AKA

YOU WON'T DO WHAT YOU CAN'T IMAGINE DOING

Vague ideas are very difficult to implement. Without a picture on the box, a jigsaw puzzle is much harder to put together. So, on the assumption that you've honed in on what you really want and why, you'll have the big picture by now. Something to aim towards and several specific milestones that mark your progress, will go a long way to getting you there.

As stated previously, there are always at least two sides to everything in a three-dimensional universe. If you have a one-sided view, the side you see is the side your reality is based upon. Seeing yourself as a gold medal winner or a gold medal loser are both possible to envision. Clearly, seeing yourself in the best possible light will be more conducive to feeling good about yourself. Seeing something as possible will be a great deal more motivating than imagining that it is impossible.

Seeing the right reward or the perfect punishment will impact you in the right way. Your outlook, view, or perspective hold great power over your experience. Feeling as if you get to do something you enjoy is much different from feeling as if you've got to do something you are dreading. Singing because you love singing, and being pressured into singing because you arrived late for a meeting, both involve singing, but the degree of stress and anxiety experienced could differ greatly.

Same thing with flying on planes. You could imagine feeling safe in the air, but if your habit is to think of air flight as terrifying, forcing yourself to do it will never be enjoyable. Your imagination, like fire and water, can be used for both good or evil. Think of lifesaving water given to someone dehydrating, or the life-taking water someone could be submerged in while drowning. The warmth of a crackling campfire or the engulfing blaze of a four-alarm house fire. Fire and water are neither all good nor all bad, and neither is your imagination.

You can imagine the best or imagine the worst, but whatever you *do* imagine will influence how you feel. You can imagine yourself as capable, or see yourself as incapable. Either way, the images you entertain in your mind will hold great sway over your state. Self-fulfilling prophecies don't all come from telling ourselves what will happen, they also come from whatever images we are holding in our minds. If you see failure as inevitable, what would be the point of trying to succeed?

IT DEPENDS ON HOW YOU SEE THINGS

The more optimistically you can look at things, the more positive you will feel as a consequence. You don't need rose-coloured glasses, but you will benefit from taking off any dirty lenses that muddy your vision and cloud your view if you want to see clearly without negative bias. Your habitual way of perceiving is another habit that was somehow learned, and thanks to neuroscience we know that it can be unlearned. You can develop a better outlook, and that different way of seeing things would translate into a different end result.

If you are going to entertain ideas in your mind, why not make them encouraging rather than discouraging? It's really all mental rehearsal, when you think about it. Why not rehearse things going the way you'd hope, rather than the way you'd fear? You are not likely to accomplish what you imagine to be impossible, but if you can imagine being able to do something, it's far likelier that you'll get around to achieving it.

Imagining the good that will come from succeeding, and the tangible benefits of achieving your goal, are both proven to be better methods of motivating yourself than just picturing what you want. You've got to be moved by the ideas held in your mind to influence your behaviour. When it comes to irrational fears and phobias, it is not the plane or the spider that the fearful phobic is scared of, it's the idea about planes or spiders that they hold in their mind. Planes crashing and burning, and spiders creeping and crawling are what moves them, not so much static ideas or statistics.

Remember the juicy lemon exercise from the previous chapter? Well there was no lemon, and yet the idea of interacting with a lemon that you entertained in your mind, caused your mouth to actually salivate. You were picturing a lemon in your mind's eye, and so I could have waited until this chapter on envisioning to introduce the lemon exercise. Since you had to reference the idea of "lemon" from your memory banks to know how to respond accordingly, I decided that it fit equally well in the conditioning chapter. You can feel free to repeat it now if you need reminding how impactful envisioning an idea in your mind can be in stimulating a response. But if you do not see that as useful, let's repeat the pendulum exercise instead, with a twist (no lemon required).

ENVISIONING EXERCISE #1

IMAGES INTO MOTION

1. Go grab the same pendulum, necklace or weighted string you used to explore the power of your mind to make movement from a couple of chapters ago. If you did not bother to do the exercise, consider taking this book and your intentions more seriously and stop telling yourself that you do not have to make any effort.

2. With the weight hanging again about 6"-8" from your thumb and fingers of the hand holding the other end, place your elbow on the arm of a chair and stare once more at the weighted end.

3. This time, picture the pendulum moving forwards and backwards in your mind. Keep envisioning it moving while you continue to stare at the pendulum.

4. As before, it can help to "want" the pendulum to respond to you. Once again, please make sure that you are not resisting in any way, any of the movements that will naturally occur if you are taking this seriously (and not imagining failure in your head).

5. Once your imagining of back and forth movements has succeeded in causing the pendulum to respond, change the image in your mind to sideways movements, and then finally circles. It will make a difference whether you see the circular movements as clockwise or counterclockwise, so you might wish to experiment with both directions.

Why did I get you to do that exercise twice, you might wonder? Well, words are one thing and pictures are another thing altogether. You can be affected by both in varying degrees. You may a have preferred representation systems (a sense you prioritize) and I wanted you to see if the words or the pictures moved your pendulum more. Knowing what worked best for you will help you save time in overinvesting too much energy in one technique when another technique clearly works better for you. You need to focus the bulk of your intending energy on whatever techniques work best for you. Feel free to combine as many techniques and senses as you like, so long as you avoid overwhelming yourself.

IMAGINATION ALWAYS WINS

If you imagined that neither of the pendulum exercises were worth doing, then you are living proof that your imagination holds great sway over you. If you were curious to discover what your mind was capable of imagining into being, doubtless you are also convinced now that whatever you imagine has a powerful impact over your experience of reality. Remember the great quote from John Henry Ford: "Whether you imagine you can or you imagine you can't, you are right." Well, Émile Coué has often been quoted as saying: "When the imagination and will are in conflict, are antagonistic, it is always imagination which wins, without any exception."

We could simplify that statement to: "When imagination and will are opposed, imagination always wins". Regardless of their exact words, both these great men and many others understand that what you imagine has the capacity to be manifested, and what you cannot imagine is unlikely to become your reality. If you'd like to shed some pounds but cannot see yourself as a slimmer version of you, you are probably not going to bother giving weight loss a serious attempt. If you cannot even imagine walking past the cake platter at a buffet to fill your dish with fresh fruit from the next display, cake is what you'll probably eat your fill of.

THE KEY TO GETTING AND STAYING MOTIVATED

It's so very important to appeal to your imagination in whatever behaviour change you are attempting to take on that will lead you to attaining your goal, simply because of the power that your imagination holds over your actions. Where words can appeal to your logical and linguistic left brain, imagined images appeal far more to your emotional and creative right brain. The combination is a good spread of your bets, but your right hemisphere has a bigger influence over your feelings and therefore your motivation. Telling yourself not to get tense when you a watching a horror film will not stop subconscious tension creeping over you, unless you are supremely reassured by mere words alone.

The impact of compelling ideas held in our minds visually, would take a thousand words to overcome, if that were even possible. Your dreams are visual and laden with impactful "symbology" – often consciously confusing pictures and movies that play in your mind that we absolutely understand unconsciously. Dream content is illustrative of the way that meaning can be projected into feeling-provoking visual ideas.

If you see yourself as powerful in your dreams, that's a great indication that you really feel resourceful and impactful in real life. See yourself falling or failing to run in quicksand in a dream, and your fears of not having control or feeling ineffective in reality, are likely being expressed by your subconscious mind. Your subconscious uses imagery to communicate to your conscious mind. It can also work the other way around if you want to impress an idea into your subconscious mind.

Working on your deep, subconscious self-image is a great way to influence how you feel about yourself on the surface. Repeatedly imagining a slim, strong, powerful and successful you, would send very positive signals to your deeper mind about how you'd like to feel in the outside world. Seeing yourself doing what you'd need to be doing to develop those qualities would be even more useful. I recommend doing that more than once, and so does science.

MONKEY DO, MONKEY FEEL

How you act will impact how you feel. See yourself acting the way you need to behave in order to succeed, and you'll soon feel better about your abilities and begin to see the results of your actions. Your subconscious self-image greatly influences your actions. Research might be inconclusive about the impact of playing violent video games on the lives and minds of gamers, but we only need to look at the history of G.I Joe and Barbie to see the impact of imagining oneself as an avatar on the psyche.

The whole point of toys like those, is to appeal to the desires of imaginative minds. They allow children to live out fantasies and picture themselves as the figurine that they were playing with. A young girl playing with the vicarious idea of Barbie getting married in a wedding dress, sets her up somewhat for the ideas about weddings and marriage that she will later be referencing as an adult. Even if she is unaware of the influence on the surface, years later, what lurks in the back of her mind will remain there, unless challenged.

Since we are comparative by nature, toying with ideas that cannot possibly be lived up to tends to smack us in the face with an unpleasant reality. Self-image issues and eating disorders have long been associated with girls comparing themselves to Barbie's impossible proportions. The same is true of G.I. Joe and boys, albeit much less publicized.

Our time spent in imaginative play is a precursor to our playing in real life. I don't believe in zombies, but if in the highly unlikely event of an actual zombie apocalypse, I'd be hiding behind any gamer I could find who'd already logged in hundreds or thousands of hours of killing zombies from their game console. Shooting deranged creatures might not be proven to make gamers more violent in real life, but if playing the part of a zombie killer every night after school wouldn't give them a better shot at defending themselves from brain eating maniacs, what is the point of a flight simulator?

Virtual reality has been shown to be profoundly impactful in teaching people to feel more confident in anxiety provoking situations, like being at the top of a tall building looking over the edge. Computer-generated flight simulators are a proven way to accelerate the process of learning to fly a plane. It might not be the same thing, but it's a great deal closer to the act of flying a plane than not engaging with the idea of controlling a plane at all. Virtual airtime increases piloting confidence and reduces the anxiety of inexperience. What we can imagine doing is certainly an influence on us, and seeing yourself failing or succeeding in whatever you want to achieve will impact you.

If you like to make vision boards and pin compelling lures and rewards in front of you on a cork board above your desk, try envisioning yourself in the images. See yourself enjoying your coveted items, don't just plonk them in front of you without engaging with the images. Picturing wonderful things you'd like to own might feel good, but it will be relatively pointless unless you are placing yourself in the picture and envisioning the joys and benefits of having them. Two Barbies on a shelf you never hold, are worth much less than the one you are playing with in your hand. Simply seeing yourself as a desirable avatar of accomplishment, like an idolized high achiever, is never going to be as effective as imagining yourself doing what they did in order to achieve the success they have.

Play leads to learning, so let yourself have fun imagining your steps to success in the theatre of your mind. Unless you are visiting a specialist like myself to help you do it more effectively, the entrance fee to enter the theatre is nonexistent. But the benefits and rewards of figuring out an action plan that you can vividly see in your mind's eye, will have a priceless payoff in your external reality.

ENVISIONING EXERCISE #2

SEEING A DIFFERENCE

1. Read through the following instructions first. Then, sitting
    somewhere safe, shut your eyes, close your eyelids and take
    two or three deep breaths, exhaling more slowly than you
    inhale. You'll also find this exercise online if you'd prefer
    to listen to me talk you through the process.

2. Bring to mind an image of yourself as you'd look hav-
    ing achieved your goal. Note any perceivable differences
    between that version of you, and the way you currently
    picture yourself. Are you happier, healthier, wealthier, or
    more attractive? Do you breathe easier, dress better, smile
    more or stand differently?

3. Wonder for a little while about what kind of things must
    have happened for you to become that you. Did you work
    out daily, say "no" to junk food, spend more time with
    loved ones or invest more energy into your business? Liter-
    ally ask yourself "What actions do I take to become this
    highly desirable me?" and passively allow any ideas and
    images to enter your mind.

4. Spend a little time entertaining yourself with the ideas
    that come to you and see yourself making the behavioural
    changes that look as if they'll lead you there. Don't rush
    this, but if you have a short attention span, do it multiple
    times to make sure you give yourself enough accumulated
    time to learn from your purposeful mind-play.

If you do not find that exercise remotely motivating, you might want to go back to your goal setting exercise. Think again about the reasons you thought would compel you to turn your big dream into a reality. If you genuinely want to succeed with your action plan, imagining hitting the milestones should get you somewhat excited. People who are phobic of spiders can literally freak themselves out simply by imagining a spider in front of them, let alone have an actual one crawling on their hand. Imagining a dark basement or attic full of spiders will make the task of digging out a box of old photos much less appealing, if not impossible to perform.

What we spend time imagining, has a powerful influence over how we feel, and in turn, how we act. Your brain does an amazing job of facilitating imagined ideas in your mind that are often only loosely based on reality. The truth is, that even though you are seeing these words on this page, your experience of them is entirely in your head. Your eyes are receptive to light from outside, and the signals sent to your brain form images in the theatre of your mind. You do not actually see reality *per se*. You see your mind's interpretation of reality, projected onto the theatre of your mind, in glorious high definition and five-sensory surround.

SEEING IS BELIEVING

The light-based images your eyes send to your brain are upside down and require being inverted using brainpower. The perceptual adaptation can be proven by hanging upside down until your brain stops inverting the already seen as upside down world, and you see things the way your inverting eyes capture it, which would now be right side up. The downsides of doing that, are both the rush of blood that would fill your brain, and the days of hanging upside down it can take to trick your mind into making the adjustment. For these reasons, I'm not suggesting doing it, but I am going to suggest a much simpler way of discovering another way that your brain makes adjustments that you might be unaware of.

I'm sure you understand the concept of a blind spot when it comes to reversing your car using only your mirrors. But are you aware that there are blind spots in your vision where the optic nerve connects to your retina? Unlike the retina, there are no photoreceptors in the optic nerve (no rods and no cones). This means that a small portion of your vision is blinded by the area of retina that is obscured by the optic nerve connection.

If you were unaware of this blind spot, that's because you've never seen anything missing from your vision. Your brain simply hallucinates what it expects to see in the area of missing sensory data. Yes folks, you read that correctly – you are hallucinating something in your periphery right now and the following exercise will prove that to you. It's also going to prove the power of expectation to you, but you might find that harder to see.

ENVISIONING EXERCISE #3

SEEING YOUR BLINDSPOT

1. Hold this book so that the following Blindspot Detector is centrally positioned between your left and right eyes, about 2" – 8" away from your face. (Digital readers may experience a different tolerance band depending on how big this book appears onscreen.)

2. Cover or close your left eye and stare over at the plus on the left with your right eye. You'll notice the minus sign in your periphery but keep looking only at the plus. No peeking!

3. Slowly and carefully, bring the page closer to, or further away from your face until the minus on the right disappears. If you are patient and you get the distance right and hold it there, you should be able to move the book to the left and right a bit without the minus reappearing.

4. In the place of the missing minus symbol, your brain will have hallucinated white space. It will also have deleted an element of your peripheral experience, demonstrating just how easy it is to lose sight of things that you are not focusing on.

5. Not impressed with that? Switch eyes and stare at the minus with your left eye having closed your right eye, and again find the distance from your face where the plus symbol disappears this time.

6. Now you will be staring at a black space that your brain is hallucinating on this white paged book. Is that more impressive?

BLINDSPOT DETECTOR

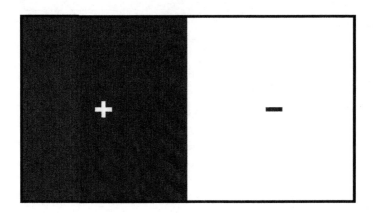

YOU CAN EASILY LOSE SIGHT OF WHAT YOU AREN'T FOCUSED ON

That exercise, when done correctly, illustrates a fascinating concept. Namely that what appears to be, might only be imagined. That whatever you *expect* to see, will be what you **do** see. When the dark negative disappeared, all you saw was light space. When the bright positive vanished, all you could see was darkness. I'm not sure if it was obvious to you without me making it clear, but the positive and negative symbols (the + and −), along with the black and white spaces, also serve as metaphors. Can you think which ones?

Seeing the positive or seeing the negative can represent the habits of optimism and pessimism, but that's not all. I'll make it even clearer for you: you could easily lose sight of your goals and the steps to get you there if you don't do something to keep them in view. Clearer now?

Whatever you see in your mind is only a representation of reality. If your representation is negative, you will be influenced by your habitual way of seeing things, to miss the positive. If your perspective is more positive, you'll more likely see obstacles as opportunities and the light at the end of every tunnel.

Your mind is hallucinating a great deal more than you might think. Science tells us that we are able to focus in detail on a very small area about the size of your thumbnail. The small area of the eye that supplies detail to the brain is called the fovea. It contains the greatest density of light receptive cells and is responsible for high definition vision. Outside of that foveal focus, your peripheral content (as provided by your lower cell density perifovea) can very easily be constructed, destructed or distorted by your mind. Strangers out the corner of our eye can be mistaken for friends and loved ones. Words on signs you aren't staring at can be made meaningless or even dissolve from consciousness, and the goals you aren't actively focusing on can disappear if you are not careful.

The reality you experience is highly subjective. It is heavily influenced by what you expect to experience, and your mind can definitely play tricks on you. I've had a few surprising and stimulating visual experiences that have solidified for me the potential the mind has to manufacture expectations. My first encounter was as a small child, waking in the middle of the night to see a squirrel run across my bed and jump out my bedroom window. A quick scream for my dad and a flick of the light switch revealed that my window was locked and no tree-rats were under my bed. I clearly recall how vividly real it seemed at the time, but then things we imagine whilst half asleep, can be incredibly real in the moment.

Decades later in Canada, I was disturbed to see a seagull writhing in agony in the middle of the road on my way to the bank. It was obvious that it had been run over. Its wing was flapping as its mangled body caused my body to recoil in empathy for the poor white bird. I could barely look at it as I drove by, making sure that I did not carelessly add to its unbearable pain. Whilst deciding if I should stop the car and offer it a quick end or a warm place to die slowly, I had to laugh at myself when it turned out to be a white plastic bag flapping in the wind! Prior to the close-up examination, I would have argued with anyone that tried to convince me that it wasn't a seagull. I don't feel silly for not seeing it as a bag, I feel amazed that my mind added so much disturbing detail.

SPOT THE DIFFERENCE

My favourite hallucinatory episode happened a couple of years ago while I was at the bathroom sink brushing my teeth. I'll never forget seeing my Persian cat sitting by the door watching me. He has a sweet little face and cute white paws that I clearly saw out the side of my gaze. As I turned to tell him what a cute, teddy bear of a pussycat he was, he pixelated in front of my eyes and turned into a smelly pair of running shoes! It was the most fascinating sight to see the transformation happen and gave me a little "wow" feeling inside. I wasn't shocked however, because I'm aware that things are not always as they seem—even if you are *certain* that you are seeing clearly.

If you drive, you've probably had the experience of searching everywhere for your car keys at some point, only to find them eventually in the first place you'd looked for them. If you don't drive, you've done it with your door key, your watch, or a pair of earrings. Negative hallucinations don't require you to be in a formal hypnotic trance to take effect, they can happen anytime and anywhere. These days, if I find myself fretting, telling myself "I can't find my keys," I swiftly shift my thinking into "I CAN find my keys" and more often than not, they suddenly appear. Either in my mind's eye to tip me off to their location, or sometimes right in front of my eyes, just to the left or right of where I was staring hard to find them.

Although this chapter is about envisioning or visualizing, it isn't only your visual senses that can be tricked peripherally. Ever been watching a TV show and heard your phone buzz or a text come in, only to find out that no call and no text were received? Ever thought you could smell gas, only to find that there was no gas leak? Felt an ant or spider on your hand or leg sometime, and then realized nothing was actually there? Just watching ants crawling over someone can creep us out and make us itch. Where do you notice that itchy sensation right now? On your nose, or cheek, or chin maybe? Or possibly a location on your body or the back of your head?

Imagination really is an amazing thing that can literally make us react to provocative ideas of all kinds. British comedy hypnotist Jonathan Chase is famous for having hypnotized tens of thousands of volunteers on stage into believing that the raw onion they were devouring, was a juicy apple! Most of them were convinced enough to argue if anyone suggested otherwise.

Crunching into an apple or an onion might sound the same, but the taste, the sight, the smell and even the texture of the onion, are all different and were all manipulated into an apple inside the minds of Jon's hypnotized volunteers. "Sensualizing" is a much better word than merely visualizing, since imagining something in all five senses makes it five times more real, if not more. Envisioning works for me, since I think you can envision the smell of an apple better than you can visualize it? But then, the words are much less important than what you are experiencing in your mind's eye (or ear, mouth, nose or fingers).

Now, it's one thing to imagine being successful at something you'd love to be successful at, but if all you ever did was imagine that you were successful, what would compel you to take any action to make it happen? Success science makes it clear to us that if you only engage in the imaginative act of envisioning yourself as already successful, it would actually have a detrimental impact on your tangible achievements. Since your neurology cannot tell the difference between what is real and what is vividly imagined, if you trick your neurology into making you feel that you've already accomplished your big dream or daily goals, you are not likely to do any of the work involved in making them actually happen.

If in the future you might regret not trying to acquire or achieve something, unless you have a time machine, you will not be able to go back and give it a go. As of writing this book there are no time machines in reality, but you don't need a time machine to imagine a future regret and then come back to the present and take action. What do you want to be remembered for, when all is said and done? Imagining what people will remember about you when you are gone is another fine way to use your imagined future to impact your real now.

In the next chapter, we are going to look at some of the ways that you can significantly increase your chances of doing what needs to get done and avoid the pitfalls of well intended people that accidentally undermine their own great goals by following popular, but ineffective advice. So, let's get back to the real world and start to get real about making your dreams a reality, as soon as we've taken stock of some of this chapter's takeaways:

CHAPTER 7 SUMMARY

AKA:

WHAT YOU'VE LEARNED BY READING THIS CHAPTER

1. How you see yourself in relation to your goal, will influence how you behave towards it.

2. Imagination always wins over willpower, so make sure you spend time mentally rehearsing success in your head.

3. Ideas that you vividly imagine cause responses in your body and behaviour.

4. If you cannot imagine doing something, you probably won't do it.

5. You see with your mind, never with your eyes. And your mind can play tricks on you – so get it to work to your advantage!

DAVID FAIRWEATHER

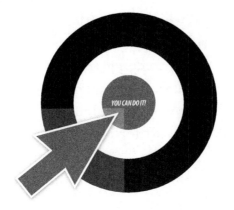

CHAPTER 8

RECORDING YOUR GOALS

AKA

TRAINING YOUR BRAIN AND
TRACKING YOUR PROGRESS

When I decided to write this book, I began plotting how it could be accomplished in six weeks. I'm not saying that I believed it could be planned, researched, written, proofread, edited, illustrated, formatted, reviewed and published in print in that time whilst continuing to see coaching clients and accepting speaking engagements. But I wanted a goal that I could take aim at and see how close to the target my efforts would land. Each and every day, I would read over the previous day's work. Each and every week, I assessed my progress and reassessed where my best efforts should be channeled to keep me on track as much as possible.

I found it encouraging to see the progress I was making and sometimes discouraged when I made the mistake of focusing on what I had yet to write or had not yet accomplished. A whole book is a big deal, but by keeping track of the two chapters a week I'd set myself the task of completing, I gave myself some necessary pressure. It was not a ridiculous amount of pressure, but I certainly could not slack off for more than a day here or there, without setting myself up for a more immense and unpleasant amount of pressure to compensate for an unproductive down-day.

It's supremely important to take stock from time to time about your progress, otherwise you'll remain delightfully delusional about not being off course. It might be nice not knowing how far behind you are getting, but it's much more useful getting real with yourself about the reality of your efforts. The simplest method of doing that is to simply keep a log of doing them. A page of empty, dated tick boxes is something I personally like to use, but you might prefer putting them into your personal scheduler, digital to-do list or smartphone.

Regular reviews, assessments and reassessments are vital to conduct if you are serious about being successful. One of the best ways of ensuring that you don't fall off the progress wagon into wishful thinking, is a weekly review of what did, and what did not get done. It's not so much what did not get done, so much as what did not get done that you had planned to do on deadline.

Doing things that you hadn't planned as a vehicle for feeling productive is another problem entirely. If you have a plan, you are going to need to follow it—unless you made a poor plan. If the plan isn't realistic, change it. That is entirely the point of a weekly check-in. By looking at what is and what isn't working, you can make course-correcting adjustments long before you find yourself miles or months off-target.

Every good coach will tell you that "What gets tracked, gets done," because they know it's true. Convince yourself otherwise, and you've opened a loophole that will not lead you anywhere worth arriving. So, whether you use empty tick boxes that goad you into checking them off, or a structured, solution-focused approach to journalling, putting pen to paper will pay off in the long run. Assessing how well you hit your targets and figuring out how to overcome any recently discovered obstacles, will keep your brain aimed at succeeding. Simply noting how badly you performed this past week might only serve to discourage you.

A weekly review will not only help you to see the progress you've made and aid you in feeling good about your efforts to accomplish something desirable to achieve, it will also give you a chance to set your new goals for the following week based on your current reality. Once you've written out an updated set of goals for the week to come, it's a good idea to read them out loud to yourself and affirm your intention to get them done.

I tend to write myself a set of objectives to accomplish every single day. But without referencing your weekly targets, doing that could result in feeling busy just doing "stuff". The stuff you do every day simply has to be relevant to your weekly agenda, which in turn must respect your mid-range goals, or you'll only be busy being busy. You need to be busy being successful.

DON'T LOSE SIGHT OF YOUR GOALS

Once you've written out your directives for the day, you might want to make a point of making sure that you see them regularly. Placing sticky notes on the mirror in your bathroom or on your computer screen, are both great ways to keep yourself focused on what really needs to get done. Of course, put too many notes up and you could find them an overwhelming distraction. You might even habituate to them, allowing them to fade from your awareness by seeing them in front of you too often and not connecting with their pertinent messages. We are prone to ignoring what is always in front of us. Don't let your collage of notes become wallpaper patterns that you no longer really notice.

You are not going to feel propelled into action by anything that blends in with your environment. If you no longer smell the pickled herring rotting behind your fridge, pungent though it was, your habituated noseblindness will have numbed you from noticing. Spend a little while away from home and you could be surprised how much odour your subconscious mind had blocked out. After a while, even a dark room seems less dark as you habituate to darkness and notice the darkness less. What you do not notice will go unnoticed.

Just because something isn't noticed, it doesn't mean that it doesn't affect you. Some people block the sight and smell of black mold out until they eventually become sick as a result. Subliminal influence is a far cry from toxic bacteria, but both can impact you massively without your conscious involvement.

We've already looked at the subliminal influence that advertisers capitalize on by having their jingles and messaging forming the background soundscape of your day. A powerful thing that you can do to get your goals etched into your mind like a master marketer's mesmerizing message, is to record your goals being spoken out loud and to play them back to yourself. You do not even have to pay attention to them for them to sink into your skull and influence you.

Doubt that? The average North American knows the tag lines of many more commercials than they think they do. It's fun pointing this out from the stage whilst addressing audiences of entrepreneurs and sales agents that can effortlessly join in with the deceptively silly jingles they've subconsciously absorbed off the TV and radio.

• "Have a break, have a ___ ___."

• "It takes a lickin' and _____ __ _____."

• "Let your fingers __ ___ _____."

In Canada, we have:

• "Always got time for ___ _____"

• "It was a rainy day in _____"

• "Everyone loves _____ ____"

The list of memorable marketing messages, products and services that consumers have all absorbed and internalized, is surprisingly long. But they all have one thing in common: no one has ever invested any effort whatsoever in committing any of them to memory! Even the voice artists were reading from scripts when they were recorded. They've just played over and over in the background of your life, and yet almost every sentient citizen knows them off by heart. Your heart beats without having to think about it, and memorable messages roll out of your head and off your tongue effortlessly (without having to think about it).

Even hearing the words of a memorable slogan or catchphrase can immediately put the product or service that they are connected to in your head. As an example, Ikea's "Start the Car" commercial may have been chosen by TIFF as one of the top ten most influential adverts in Canadian history, but to me it has forever ruined that once benign phrase! I cannot even imagine hearing those words without replaying the screech of the actor's voice grating on my brain. It's an awesome piece of marketing, even if it is the single most irritating advert I've ever been subjected to. It might be so awesome because it's so annoying, since strong emotions burn in memories. I know I'm unlikely to ever forget it.

Consider committing your self-marketing messages to memory by recording them, and playing them back to yourself while you do your filing, answer emails, tidy your office, fill out your time sheets, sit on the throne, eat your breakfast, or drive to work or school. You'll be doing those things regularly anyway, so if you make it a habit to play a sound file listing off your trackable activities and mission messages, whenever you do them, you'll being doing way more than the average person bothers doing, and it will be almost effortless.

YOUR INTERNAL ALERT SYSTEM

As brought to your attention previously, your reticular activation system determines what filters up into your conscious awareness, determined by what is important to you. Because of that, consistent engagement with any idea will be programming your RAS with information about what to look out for. So, if you are listening daily to a recording that is focused on ideas about your ideal food choices, or the characteristics of your ideal client, those top of mind concepts will tend to be brought to your conscious attention automatically and without any effort on your part. If you've built in a contextual component like, "Whenever I enter a networking meeting…" or "When I am in the grocery store…." your RAS will know exactly when to bring the recorded suggestions to your attention.

This deceptively simple technique is one of the easiest psychological hijacks of human nature that you can invest a little time into accomplishing in pursuit of your success. It works best by spacing messages out in a sound file so that they play back like separate statements interspersed with silent pauses. With little spaces between statements, the phrases won't all blur into a barrage of words like a book on tape that requires your attention to make sense of. You aren't looking to make sense of them, you are seeking to let them seep deep into your neurology where they can influence you subconsciously.

Passive repetition is a super human-programming device, used to diabolical effectiveness by profit-driven companies who want their products and services to be top of mind. So why not take advantage of your capacity to mindlessly learn, and make yourself a commercial for your own success? Your mission statements don't have to rhyme, but if they do, even better!

Recording yourself voicing your elevator pitch, mission statement, big juicy goals and even your mid-range targets, would be an excellent tool for brainwashing yourself (in a good way). Playing soft instrumental music in the background while recording your voice, has been shown in studies to influence their effectiveness, but songs with words will distract you. Classical music is often cited as the most effective learning aid, so you can't go wrong with anything by Bach, Beethoven, Brahms and Mozart.

Don't own any classical music? There are plenty of classical music stations you could tune into whilst laying down your goals. But avoid stations that involve a lot of DJ chatter and definitely stay away from those that pump out adverts frequently between the tunes. The 1812 overture is to be avoided, thanks to the alarming cannons. And I'd swerve any marches that pump you up instead of relaxing your neurology and opening your mind. J.S Bach's Largo from Concerto in G Minor for flute and strings, and Wolfgang Amadeus Mozart's Piano Concerto No. 23 are both excellent examples of the kind of soothing instrumentals that are perfect for playing in the background as you record your personal motivational aid.

GET YOURSELF MOVING

Thanks to smart phones these days, you don't even need a voice recorder to set your intentions down in an audible form. Every phone has a voice memo app, and that is already in your pocket or purse and ready to get to work for you. When it comes to the actual recording, leave a little space at the beginning and end of your sound file where only music plays. This will give you time to settle into your attention absorbing task before the subliminal messages enter sonically into the sound waves around you.

Not everyone likes to hear their voice play back to them, so it might take a little getting used to. I recommend not paying attention! If you find that impossible to do, you are listening way too consciously for subliminal learning to take place, so you should certainly stop doing that and focus on your distracting task at hand.

Using your own voice makes it easy for you to even record your daily goals each week, if you want. You also get to read them out as convincingly as possible with congruent conviction. If you struggle with that, you might consider accepting a challenge from me to record believable takes of your goal affirming statements, and that can really help you get congruent about your conviction. However, I'm not trying to torture you with this advice, so I'm not closed off to you utilizing an online voice artist to read them out over some Mozart for you.

There is an entire online industry of people prepared to record voiceovers for whiteboard animations and promotional videos, that charge quite reasonably for their services. Of course, their voices, accents and energy are all different, so if you are considering outsourcing your motivational audio recording, please choose someone based on results, not cost. A poorly delivered message probably won't inspire you in the same way that a professional voiceover artist's compelling statements could. An unconvincing voice has the power to kill the most inspirational message, so pick someone that already has several great examples of their work for you to listen to.

IF YOU WANT A JOB DONE WELL

I can't say that your voice is any better or worse than someone else's, but I do know that what you believe is the most important aspect of any audio you invest time in listening to. You must be able to believe it. If you respond better to encouragement from others, and you like hearing someone else telling you what you think and how you behave, then hiring someone to record your message for you is probably your best option. If, like me, you prefer taking orders from yourself and not other people, go with your own voice and get used to it.

It shouldn't take you very long to set your self-propelling statements to a sound file. Maybe fifteen to thirty minutes, tops. Once it's done, you'll be able to listen to your goal-affirming messages, agreed-upon commitments, and stimulating visual convincers, over and over and over again. How much you will need to listen, is going to depend on your current level of motivation and the length, complexity and emotional intensity of the statements. How open your mind is to agreeing with, or believing the messages, is also going to be a factor.

A tall bottle with a small opening takes longer to fill than a wide jar with a large opening. Even if they both hold a litre of fluid, the smaller opening of a tall bottle will slow the process of adding liquid, and a wide mouth mason jar will permit a quick filling in much less time. Your mind may not be a glass vessel, but it is a container. Your mind is a container of beliefs and memories. Memories are formed from emotional moments, and the stronger the emotion experienced in the moment, the more likely you are to never forget it.

Having said that, we are certainly capable of remembering some relatively unemotional things, like numbers and dry facts. The rub is, that the more uninspiring something is, the more repetitions in working memory it will take to get it to sink in. It was for this reason that I was awarded a gold star early on at school for every times table I was able to commit to memory. Thanks to that experience, I now know that five fives are twenty-five and that six sixes are thirty-six. Of course, these days I can just consult my smartphone, which is why I have no idea what fifteen thirteens are without it.

Should I ever develop the need to program the thirteen times table into my brain, repetition would be the method of choice for committing it to memory. Better yet, would be repeatedly watching a video animation of all the various groupings of thirteen, that I could also process visually along with the spoken statements. As we've established, there are only three primary pathways to get anything burned into your brain, and the more of them you utilize, the more efficiently you are likely to learn.

To help clarify how you can get your goals recorded and turned into a Self-Propelling Sound-File™ ASAP, here are the simple steps to follow:

MOTIVATING YOUR OWN MOTION

1. Invest ten to twenty minutes today in writing out some motivating statements and reminders of what you feel you really need to be doing, why it would be beneficial for you to be doing it, and how would feel to be doing it with ease? Paint a vivid picture for yourself that is moving to you. Don't waste words aimlessly throwing facts about and avoid any negative or self-scolding statements.

2. Then I'd like you to record those personal mission statements and alluring activity primers over and over onto your smartphone until you have a five to ten minute voice recording. If there is classical music playing in the background, even better.

3. All that is left to do then, is spend a couple of minutes converting that sound file into a format you can easily play in the car on your drive to work or as you do some other daily activity.

4. That's all. Well, that and just playing it daily for at least one month without exerting any effort to pay attention to it whatsoever.

While I was recovering from my dalliance with burnout, I got a great deal of comfort and inspiration from recording my self-improvement goals regularly and listening to them daily. I had a goal to relax, a goal to breathe deeper, a goal of thinking uplifting thoughts, and goals for my physiotherapy. In times of struggle and personal need, it's good to keep focused on the positive, so you don't get bogged down or swept away by depressing thoughts. Diligently reminding yourself of the light at the end of the tunnel can keep you from falling into the arms of despair. I highly recommend it!

MONKEY SEE CLEARLY, MONKEY DO BETTER

While working at York University on a research program dedicated to increasing cultural competence in Canada amongst nurses originally educated elsewhere, we found that pictures painted far more than a thousand words. Tasked with producing educational films for the nurses to watch, our team scripted short vignettes of how things could go and how things should go within our hospital system. I got to direct acting students enacting the various scenes in our mock hospital, and then edit the footage into short, compelling movies.

Being able to watch the kinds of mistakes that could be made, followed by a version of the scenario that presented them with more ideal responses and outcomes, made it easy for the nurses to understand. The visually stimulating movies were much more memorable than paragraphs in a textbook.

In the past, I've often suggested in my psychotherapy practice that patients and clients capture their own memorable home movies of themselves speaking compellingly to their own smartphone's camera. I've suggested that newly minted nonsmokers filled with conviction, capture their own emotional message of abstinence by making a video recording of themselves, so that on the days they feel vulnerable to falling prey to the once-cool idea of smoking, they will benefit greatly from having made a moving selfie that speaks directly to them and literally talks them out of it.

Who better to convince the future you that you really ought not to fall back into a bad habit than the current you? Even better than a time capsule left for strangers to dig up and learn from, is a short but compelling video recording of you raving enthusiastically about the merits of being the kind of person you are convinced is best for you to be in the long run.

It costs you nothing but a few minutes, to turn your camera on yourself and tell yourself exactly what you will do and why you'll do it. Sure, you might feel silly at first, but even sillier would be losing sight of what is really important and sliding back to your old ineffective habits after having experienced so much motivation. Recording your messages in video form still covers the audio component, but the density of message contained by combining a visual element, is almost guaranteed to elicit a stronger emotional reaction than mere sound alone (if you watch it).

There really is no one better to believe than you, but don't take my word for it. If you feel strongly about not giving up on your dreams, and you want to amplify your ambition, dedication and motivation, don't just consider making a short selfie selling yourself on the habits you want to make second nature. Do it.

YOU CAN DO IT ON CAMERA

A pep talk from yourself, where you get to see the passion in your eyes and feel moved by the intensity of your own determination, is a great tool to engage with in your mission to succeed. Once you've committed your multimedia message to your smartphone's memory, you'll be able to sit back and soak it in, just like the nurses who developed a far deeper understanding of what was expected of them in a Canadian hospital.

Commissioning a humorous or stimulating white board animation of your mission statements, takes your self-marketing messages to another level entirely. It might be too much to consider doing each week for your specific daily goals, but combining habits of viewing and listening, consciously and subliminally, will give your brain multiple streams of input for it to process. Make them emotionally stimulating and you might even find yourself dreaming about imagined scenarios and how you will act if you are ever confronted with them. In the same way that children learn from play, you can learn from playing with ideas. Playing with them in your mind, playing them on your voice massage app and playing them on your own massive HD or 4K TV, or whatever you crazy kids are watching on these days.

If you've ever tried to get the attention of someone deeply engaged in a TV show, it won't come as a surprise to you that compelling TV is essentially hypnotic. It draws us into its images and ideas and even has the power to make us forget to do what we were intending to do before we got transfixed on it. However, if what we are watching is reminding us to do what we need to do, it becomes much harder to forget to do it. TV induces trances and mesmerizes its viewers into buying products we don't necessarily need, and feeling emotions communicated to us by actors and directors. Direct your own success-driving drama and act out your own compelling infomercial, and you will be delivering a powerful message to a mind wide-open and primed to absorb almost anything.

Good times to watch it would be last thing at night just before falling asleep, and first thing in the morning when your mind is at its most open. Of course, the best possible time would be around 2-3 AM when people statistically buy the most useless products off the shopping channel that they'd never normally purchase in their right mind!

Regardless of whether the delivery method is auditory or visual, the kinaesthetic feeling-state of wide openness to integrating the ideas being communicated to you, is ideal for getting the most ideas in as quickly as possible. Let's look now at how you can get yourself into a the most conducive state of mind for absorbing your own messaging as effectively and efficiently as humanly possible. We'll take a moment to go over a few significant elements of this chapter first:

CHAPTER 8 SUMMARY

AKA:

WHAT YOU'VE LEARNED BY READING THIS CHAPTER

1. Keep track of your progress regularly and be prepared for course corrections and reevaluation.

2. Make a daily agenda of the one to three most important tasks that you can complete each day.

3. Record your goals on a sound file and make a playlist or CD of them.

4. Use passive repetition to your advantage by playing the sound file over and over each day for at least a month.

5. Record a motivating message for yourself in video selfie form and make a habit of watching it last thing at night and first thing in the morning.

DAVID FAIRWEATHER

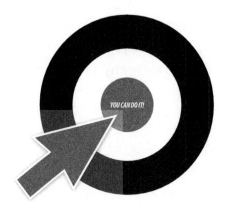

CHAPTER 9

PROGRAMMING YOURSELF TO SUCCEED

AKA

GETTING REAL ABOUT YOUR DREAMS

So far, I'm hoping you can clearly see that almost anything is possible when you set your mind to it and you don't take your eyes off the prize. Anyone can sit around daydreaming about whatever passively pops into their head, just like we can all go to the movies and let the film play. But if it was our job to know the story intimately backwards and forwards so that we could direct or promote it effectively, we'd have to develop a much deeper understanding of it than the average audience member.

When you were first born, you did a lot of sitting around letting the world play for you. You were a natural observer that sat in awe of everything in eyesight, hands reach and earshot. You'd use all your senses to explore, tasting pebbles when mother wasn't looking and smelling your own diaper until mother changed you. If she habitually changed you badly, you probably weren't critical of her, you didn't know any better yet. We learn a great deal by comparison.

You might have been uncomfortable, but you weren't able to describe what you'd prefer to be different. You didn't think thoughts at first, because you had not yet learned a language with which to form them from. It's like you existed in a perpetual daydream state, or trance, the purpose of which was to learn about the world you'd been launched into at birth. Experience is how we learn, not by being told. Unless your childhood is a sad story, your first experiences were probably of being attended to, breastfed, changed, smiled at, spoken to, kissed, tickled, loved and hugged.

If it was possible for you to think thoughts, you might have thought the world literally revolved around you. You weren't literally a sponge, but your brain was like a sponge, fascinated and open to absorbing every novel thing you experienced as you sought to make sense of everything. Your brainwaves were slow, and your reactions took time to form as you were literally mesmerized by your environment. You looked with curiosity at every new object and you didn't do a lot of knowing what everything was yet.

Your unfolding experiences were the only reality you had any awareness of, and your experiences today continue to be informed by the expectations you formed. Pebbles are still too hard to bite, and full diapers still smell like crap! You know from experience what is nice and what is nasty, what is possible and what is not possible for you to do. At least you think you know. I'm not suggesting that you should start chomping on small stones again, but I am suggesting that all the "knowing" you do isn't necessarily true, but merely a memory of what was once experienced as possible or not.

BOUND TO REPEATING HISTORY?

As we've seen, "good" things are only a perception formed around things that just are. Nothing starts off good or bad, but your initial experience of anything will tend to prejudice your expectations going forward. It is not that you cannot accomplish something that you failed to accomplish at first. Whenever we are confronted with something novel that we've yet to form a reference memory and informed opinion about, it could go either way.

Humpty Dumpty could fall to either side of the fence and wall himself off from seeing the other side of anything. Once you've made up your mind about something, all the king's horses and all the king's men would find it hard to change your perspective. It's hard to see the other side of a situation sometimes. It can be accomplished if you are open to having been wrong, and you aren't a lawyer on retainer.

An open mind, or *beginner's mind* as mindfulness practitioners call it, is an achievable state available to you if you'd like to change how you think, feel, perceive or respond to any limiting beliefs that are holding you back in life. It seems that regardless what we call that state: a learning state; a trance state; the "zone"; a flow state; beginner's mind; a state of not-knowing; being open minded; the high-performance mind; an autogenic state; a hypnotic state of mind; a daydream state, or even the "trance of infinite possibilities" as NLP trainer and hypnotic coaching guru John Overdurf calls it, there is a state of mind for human beings that is far more conducive to absorbing new experiences than a state of being a know-it-all.

Placing your expectations aside and opening your mind in an unbiased way to different perspectives is not as hard to do as you might previously have believed. You are only as locked into your beliefs as you believe you are. If you believe you cannot succeed, that is not going to be conducive to really trying. Human beings do not enjoy being proven wrong, but if you are open to being mistaken about your limitations, your open state of mind will be useful in avoiding their subconscious influence. Imagine if what you really wanted to accomplish was possible. Then keep imagining that until you achieve it!

That kind of purposeful daydreaming by itself is not necessarily going to lead you to succeed with your dreams, but it will help you to break out of the imagined belief that it is impossible for someone like you to do so. Our imagination is said to occur in the realm of alpha waves within our brains. Alpha waves are slower brainwave activity than the faster thoughts that exist at the frequency band called beta waves. Beta waves are your "internal chatter" in the form of words entertained in your head. See pictures in your mind, recall the smell of mint, or imagine the sound of the ocean, and the relevant sensory memories will play in the theatre of your mind informed by alpha waves.

Our senses are processed at a deeper level and at slower brainwave rates than the words we've learned to describe them. Regardless of the words all the king's men use to try to get Mr. Dumpty to see their perspective, it will never be the words used that could sway him to reform his opinion. It would be the ideas entertained in his head that could ultimately cause him to see the merits of their counter-argument. When you were a child and Humpty Dumpty was just an embryo, your mind was primarily filled with slow wave activity.

DEVELOPING THOUGHTS

Up until the age of 2, everything just was, and your brainwaves tranced along at about 2 cycles per second. We adults call those delta waves, but you didn't know what they were called even though your head was full of them. By the time you were about 4 years old, your brainwaves had sped up a little to around 4 cycles per second and you were oblivious that they were called theta waves. Around 8 years old, your brain was primarily dominated by alpha waves that flew by at approximately 8 cycles per second. And by the age of 16, your beta waves heavily influenced your teenage angst and far more critical thinking than a 6-year-old is capable of, at the rapid rate of approximately 16 cycles per second.

As adults, we still have the capacity to quiet the incessant beta chatter in our heads and drift into deeper experiences of alpha imagining and theta experiencing. The legendary Scottish scientist and surgeon James Braid is famous for introducing the word "hypnosis" into the English speaking world's lexicon in the 1800's. He is also famous for saying that: "Seeing is believing, but feeling is the very truth." I'd like to add that "Words are merely ways to describe what we perceive and are far removed from our true feelings".

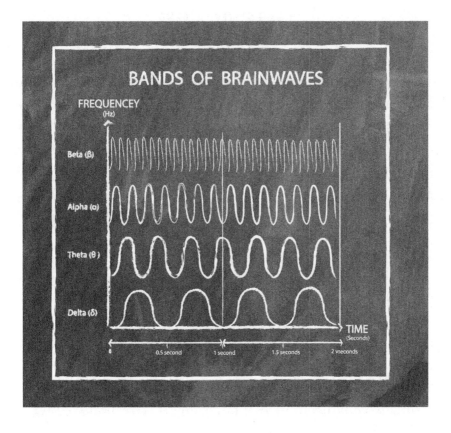

As a trainer's trainer and a practitioner of a brainwave biofeedback training protocol that has been in development since the 1970's called the Awakened Mind (aka the High-Performance Mind) training, I own technology that can be used to read minds. I can see the actual brainwave activity of anyone hooked up to sensitive EEG sensors that can represent the activity visually using a sophisticated software program called the Mind Mirror. I can map brainwave activity to the stimulus that triggered it, and I can see **how** people think, even though I cannot see *what* they are thinking.

DON'T BELIEVE A WORD

From my studies in this field and over a decade of experience as a psychotherapist and clinical hypnotist, I understand that words are beta waves, perceptions are processed in alpha waves and our reference experiences are formed in theta waves. Your beliefs are not formed in words. Words are just a conscious rationalization of what you feel or imagine. Changing deeply engrained beliefs seems to benefit from reaccessing the level of brainwave activity that was involved in encoding them into your neurology in the first place, namely alpha and theta waves.

Deep relaxation makes it much easier to access slower-wave brain activity than agitation, tension and nervousness do. Tension triggers your stress response and relief triggers your relaxation response. Feeling forced or threatened to change a deep belief, does not naturally inspire an open state of mind conducive to accepting anything that conflicts with what you are already convinced of. The polar opposite response of feeling safe to explore new ideas, and an openness to accepting that what you are learning really *is* reality, is what is required of you.

When you were a baby, you didn't question everything. You merely explored the new world with a wonderfully open state of mind. Until you knew better, you could even believe that there were monsters hiding under your bed and freak yourself out in the process. Imagination can certainly be used both positively and negatively, like fire and water. Our imagination is an amazing thing that has the power to move us if we are open to letting go of logic and getting lost in it. A refusal to allow your imagination to take control will be experienced with some degree of tension, in the same way that people telling lies are not as comfortable as open people with nothing to hide.

What you resist persists and creates tension, and what you accept is easy and effortless. Vigilant protection amplifies beta wave activity and reassured relaxation encourages alpha-theta states, which are scientifically proven to aid personal transformations of any kind. This is why autogenic relaxation, guided visualization, and whatever hypnosis is, all make reprogramming minds easier to accomplish than any arguing with words ever could. Brains saturated in alpha and theta waves, held softly in a state of imaginative absorption, are simply in the ideal condition to maximize any new learnings.

We tell children stories for a reason. Intuitively, we've understood that conjuring up ideas in the absorbent minds of a fascinated audience, appeals to their imagination much more than dry facts ever could. I've very purposefully been appealing to both your logical mind and your emotional mind throughout this book in the same way that I work hard on stage to elicit feelings from my audiences through entertaining demonstrations, not just deliver them lifeless lessons listed on a PowerPoint that are matter-of-factly referred to. I've given you things to imagine and stories to see in your head, in the hopes that whatever does not currently make sense to you, at least seems worth pursuing further, in order to understand more fully.

A RELAXING HABIT HELPS

When I worked at York University in Toronto, one of my directives was to help increase the pass rates of international nurses taking the Canadian Nurses Association bridging exam so that they were legally able to practice their vocation of nursing in our country. Their primary problem was fear of failure. The critical exam could only be retaken two times before they would be forced to give up nursing forever, or go back to their country of origin and give up their dreams of living in Canada. The stakes were huge, and their stressed-out nervous systems made it hard for them to perform at a high level, answering a question almost every minute for four continuous hours under such incredible pressure.

Stress and anxiety trigger flares of brain bashing beta waves, and soothing, sensory soundscapes, ease your mind into a relaxed openness, where appealing words can wash away any tension. For this reason, the primary intervention we offered the nurses who were open to discovering how to elicit a more conducive state of mind and body for acing exams, was delivered experientially via a sound-file. Having conducted a meta-analysis of the most effective stress – and anxiety-reduction methods from the Harvard University research archives, I devised a condensed version for our nurses, incorporating many of their best exercises for eliciting the relaxation response in the shortest amount of time.

The recording of my heavily scripted learning aid was made available to each of our willing participants and they were each tasked with figuring out which of the methods worked best for them, so that they could briefly revisit their learned relaxation state prior to putting pen to paper in any exam. The results were astounding. I also connected some of them to biofeedback equipment, so that we had plenty of tangible evidence that deeply relaxed states were being effortlessly achieved, simply by their listening along to my soothing instructions. Of course, soft music formed the background of my stress relieving sound-files.

The nurses loved listening along and felt fantastic for ages afterwards. They also began performing much better in their exams and eagerly expressed feeling immensely more confident that they could do it. They could easily pass this once ominous test, because they were no longer imagining it was the monster that threatened to end their career in nursing.

I PUT A SPELL ON YOU

When I was a young boy, my poor father had unwittingly attempted to teach me to be anxious about everything in life by demonstrating his many phobias and paranoias. He believed that big bad elevators were to be feared and that being out in the marketplace for any length of time would result in a "dizzy spell". That was quite a diabolical spell to entrance himself with, but somehow, I managed to avoid catching his agoraphobia. The spell I fell under the influence of, was instead positive and generative.

When I was around 11 or 12 years old, I was hypnotized by a gym teacher. Don't jump ahead in your mind, this is not the story you might be scared you are about to read. Rather than anything ominous, I was introduced to the power of my imagination to engage in a relaxation exercise, that I've since used hundreds, possibly thousands of times over the last four decades, whenever I've had any issue sleeping or needed to relax deeply. I can't remember the name of the teacher, and I can't say I even liked him that much, thanks to being whacked on the behind by him with a badminton racket for laughing in his class, and receiving the punishment of having to collect all the athletic equipment at the end of every P.E. lesson, simply because I didn't accept his request to join the school rugby team when they needed a good tackler.

I spent the last year of high-school avoiding him and P.E classes, but I'm happy to share with you the method of numbing a body to sleep that I was taught. It might have been his idea, but I'm happy to take credit for the following exercise as being my own, simply because after all this time, it has evolved beyond the words he must have used that I no longer recall. I've also added elements from some of the autogenic relaxation, mindfulness, meditation, and self-hypnosis courses that I've invested time in, that I believe enhance the effectiveness of the simple technique. Please be sure to read through this exercise a couple of times to understand it fully before you try it. Alternatively, you might prefer listening to me read it to you by accessing the audio version online.

So, without further ado, welcome to my Red Jelly Relaxation exercise:

RED JELLY RELAXATION

1. At a time that you have no compelling reason not to lay back and relax for a few minutes, set yourself on a supportive and comfortable surface like a recliner, a bed, or a yoga mat on the floor.

2. Uncross your arms and legs so that your feet are not touching each other and your hands rest to your sides. Use a pillow to support your head and neck if you like, but once comfortable, please avoid any further movements.

3. Close your eyes and decide that you are about to experience a wonderful sense of deep relaxation, and that if it is safe and appropriate to do so, you might even fall asleep.

4. Pool your attention on the tips of your toes and imagine to the best of your abilities, that a soothing red jelly is spreading over the ends of your feet. As the warm red jelly covers your toes, they become comfortably numb.

5. Imagine what it would feel like to anaesthetize your toes with an anaesthetic jelly that renders them warm and unable to move.

6. Allow the warm red jelly to spread deliciously across the bottom of your feet, covering the arch, the heel, and around the front of each foot and over both your ankles.

7. Wherever the jelly spreads, imagine that part of your body becoming completely immobilized during this exercise and imagine being unable to move your feet and ankles now.

8. Allow the warm red numbing jelly to make its way slowly up your legs, thoroughly warming them and rendering them comfortable and still.

9. Picture the jelly passing over your knees and be patient as it warms your thighs and reaches your pelvic area.

10. Remember, whatever parts of your body become covered completely by this numbing agent, no longer move and remain immobilized.

11. Conjure up an image of the warm red jelly spreading across your belly and lower back, while you imagine the warm sensation of tingly numbness that immobilizes your lower torso and continues to affect your legs and feet in such a comfortable way.

12. Bring the jelly up over your chest and upper back in your mind and begin picturing the jelly covering your shoulders in comfort and relaxation.

13. Imagine your arms being coated in wonderful warm red jelly and allow them to feel heavy and remain motionless as the jelly slowly covers your wrists, hands and fingers.

14. With your hands and arms resting limply at your side, imagine the jelly beginning its journey up your neck, over your chin and around the back of your head.

15. Breathing comfortably and deeply, spread the jelly over your entire skull and around your forehead and ears, all the time imagining the pleasant, warm and numbing feeling that the red jelly causes you to experience.

16. Keeping your eyes closed, imagine this lovely jelly seeping over your eyelids and comfortably caressing them in numbness, as if opening them is now no longer desirable nor possible to contemplate doing, without breaking all this wonderful relaxation.

17. Continuing to breathe comfortably, imagine that the jelly can cover your nose and nasal passages without obstructing your soothing inhalations and relaxing exhalations in any way.

18. Finally, when you are ready, allow the jelly to make its way over and around your lips, knowing all the time that breathing is easy and that the jelly in no way affects your ability to breathe out more slowly than you inhale, and you can rest in this comfortable numbness for as long as you'd like to enjoy it.

19. If sleeping is what you desire to do now, imagine beginning to dream the most wonderful dream and let your body stay still while you enjoy entering your dream fully and completely. Your dream can be related to the incredible future you wish to manifest for yourself, or simply inspire your nervous system to relax completely and benefit from a few moments of worry-free rest.

20. When you are ready to return, simply tell yourself that the jelly is about to evaporate on the count of 5, and begin energizing yourself with a count-up that incorporates an increase in the speed of your breathing and the knowledge that on the count of 5, you will open your eyes, come fully back to the room and feel fantastic!

I PUT A SPELL ON ME

I didn't know it at the time, but I believe I've actually been practicing a form of self-hypnosis since I was 11 or 12 years old. It might have been autogenic relaxation or guided meditation, there really isn't much tangible difference, even though they aren't technically the same. But one thing is for sure: the high-performance mind state that combining deep physical relaxation and purposeful daydreaming accomplishes, is a profoundly useful state of mind for anyone wishing to overcome their own mental hurdles and break down any imagined barriers that are preventing them from becoming the best version of themselves.

Some people are really bothered by the word "hypnosis" and are leery of anything remotely "hypnotic". The problem with that degree of overcaution, is that many, many things are hypnotic. Technically, only hypnotism between a hypnotist and a "hypnotee" can actually be considered hypnosis. Unlike guided visualization and purposeful daydreaming, hypnosis requires a relinquishing of control and sometimes a test of who has the power in the relationship. People are not afraid of hypnosis or hypnotists, people are afraid of not being in control.

You'll note that I did not tell you that you could not open your eyes in the previous exercise and then challenge you to prove it was impossible. In my coaching practice, I routinely engage people's imaginations, but I do not need to exert any measure of control that would push the experience into being hypnotism. I'm not trying to worry people, I'm working to relax them. Often, that is all that is needed to open their minds to changing.

If you've been taking the previous chapters seriously and completing the exercises for: establishing concrete achievable goals; deciding on the immediate gratifications you'll reward yourself with for accomplishing them; along with some self-motivating, mind-priming imagery and affirmations that will encourage your daily engagement with your success strategies, one of the best ways you can develop unwavering dedication to succeed, is to incorporate your own high-performance self-programming state into the process. The process for successfully achieving the state does benefit from biofeedback such as the Mind Mirror, a blood pressure monitor, a stress thermometer, or even inexpensive biodots that can alert you to how competently you are able to relax your mind and body. But they are not a deal breaker if you are committed to learning how to relax deeply and completely. Simplified, the process is as follows:

EXERCISES

HIGH PERFORMANCE
SELF-PROGRAMMING STEPS

1.   **RELAX** your body and mind, deeply and progressively in a comfortable chair or laying down. Allow each muscle group to progressively relax (like in the Juicy Lemon Relaxation exercise) and remain still so that all your attention can become focused within your mind. Clear your mind of any inner dialogue, thereby naturally reducing your beta wave activity.

2.   **IMAGINE** a place in your mind, ideally outside in nature and full of sensory stimulation that you can drift deeply into, as if you were really there. Imagine feeling things like the wind on your body, the ground below your feet, sea spray against your cheeks and the smell of cut grass, fresh flowers or pine needles in the air. Sense the warmth or coolness of that imagined environment and notice the sounds of birds, animals or other creatures that one would find there. This will increase your alpha wave activity and bring you into an alternate reality to the room your body is really in.

3. **TRANSFORM** your imagined reality into a deeper level of realization by walking through it. Go down hills, through garden gates, along paths, down steps and even fall softly down a rabbit hole, if the mood takes you. This will encourage theta wave activity and create the perfect state of mind for symbolizing any obstacles you'd like to symbolically overcome. In the same way that your dreaming brain engages with symbolic representations like mountains and mole-hills, imagine yourself overpowering your demons, escaping your fears, achieving your goals and FEEL-ING FANTASTIC about it!!!

REMEMBER:

IF YOU CAN'T IMAGINE DOING SOMETHING, YOU PROBABLY WON'T DO IT. YOUR IMAGINATION IS A POWERFUL FORCE – SO USE IT FOR GOOD, NOT EVIL!

LEARNING LESSONS FROM HIGH PERFORMERS

Author of *The High-Performance Mind*, Anna Wise dedicated her short but incredible life to systematizing a way that we can all gain access to our full potential, that wouldn't require purchasing the kind of sophisticated EEG equipment that I invested in years ago. Her work is definitely worth a look at, as is anything by author of *Hypnotic Realities*, Milton Erickson, probably the most credited proponent of hypnosis and self-hypnosis that has ever graced our earth. They might have differing views, since Milton believed that hypnosis was always happening everywhere, and Anna firmly believed that her methods and the methods of her teacher C. Maxwell Cade, could in no way be considered hypnosis.

I did not get to train with either of those amazing, world-class teachers, just as I never got to learn personally from psychologist Thomas Harris or Hans Selye, the Canadian scientist who put the word "stress" in the dictionary. But in my endeavours to achieve excellence in what I do, I sought to train under the best professionals that were still alive and worked with several that had been personally mentored by Erickson, Selye, Harris and Wise. Thanks to determination and a great network of incredibly supportive people, I have had the privilege of training with the personal apprentices of each of those sadly departed mega-minds of the 20th century.

Every single one of their apprentices are strong believers in both the reality and the power of hypnosis. They all have an unshakable conviction that we all have the power to access the kind of unwavering self-belief that every single one of the high performers that's been mentioned throughout these pages, has demonstrated in droves. Every person on the planet dips in and out of altering ego states, and what some would define as trances, multiple times every single day. Trance states are incredibly ordinary, as is the hypnotic learning state of increased influence. If you have children, you may have noticed how deeply immersed into video games they can effortlessly become. Try calling them for dinner and you'll often find them unresponsive.

Unless your mind is chaotically scattered, you've probably experienced being similarly engaged with a compelling book once upon a time that you did not hear someone calling you. Or, you might have read a couple of paragraphs, only to realize moments later that you were paying no attention whatsoever to whatever it was you read, and needed to go back and reread them?

You might have been so deep in thought on the drive home from work one day, that you surprised yourself by missing the enormous 12-foot sign alerting you to your exit off the highway. Or maybe you made it all the way to your driveway without any tangible recollection of most of your journey? We all drift off in our heads, entertaining daydreams and disengaging from reality much more than we are consciously aware.

In fact, if you've ever found yourself being lured into slumber by the blissful idea of falling asleep, and then suddenly jolted or jerked due to that falling feeling, you were drifting into the hypnotic state that separates waking reality from dreaming sleep, scientifically referred to as the **hypnogogic state.** Science says we pass through a hypnotic state, both on the way in and on the way out of sleep.

Regaining wakeful alertness after deep dreaming sleep, involves passing through another hypnotic state known technically as the **hypnopompic state.** The fun thing about that state is its ability to keep us believing our recent dream content is true for a little while, even though it was really only a dream. (Remember my phantom squirrel?) Everyone dreams, whether they remember their dreams or not. If you do remember your dreams, I'm sure you've awoken from a bad dream at some point, and for a little while you lay there with your eyes closed, before it dawned on you that what you were worrying about was only dream content.

Dream content has the power to persist for some time after you are technically awake, and for a short time, we really can lose touch with reality. This, for me, is essentially the state that stage hypnosis subjects are guided into, so that they can demonstrate some amazing hypnotic phenomena to audience members that often find the demonstrations too incredible to believe. Whenever I do this in a motivational presentation, I stay well away from humiliating skits and scary ideas, entertaining as our voyeuristic society tends to find the pain of others. As a licensed therapist speaking on a serious topic, I prefer to look after my on-stage daydreamers by only suggesting phenomena that I'd be happy to experience myself or subject my mum to.

Dreams are often only fleeting, but they have the power of influencing us immensely. As relieving as it is to realize that your bad dream was not real, the hypnotic states of pre – and post – slumber are fantastic states of mind in which to entertain alternate realities where you really can accomplish your big dreams and attain the accomplishments you deeply desire to make real. I highly recommend focusing on imagery related to achieving your hoped-for success as you are drifting into sleep, as you will very likely continue to entertain the ideas in your dreams once you've drifted off.

MAKE-BELIEVE UNTIL YOU MAKE BELIEF

Seeding your dreams in this way, or better yet, by listening to prerecorded, imagination-inspiring sound files before bed, is an excellent way to "make-believe" until you make belief. It's also why Émile Coué suggested repeating your affirmations twenty times, last thing at night and first thing in the morning. Your neurology cannot tell the difference between what is vividly imagined and reality. So, imagine doing what you need to do to achieve your big goal often enough, and it really will begin to feel like second nature.

Utilize a natural trance state in the process, and you will literally supercharge your determination to succeed at anything you set your mind to. One of the easiest and most effective ways of doing this, is to set your sound file as your smartphone's morning wake-up call and let your smartphone do all the work for you!

Hypnotic or not, your imagination is not something to be accessed flippantly, even though it is easy to access effortlessly. I'd never recommend engaging your imaginative mind while driving, operating heavy equipment or using a knife. Hopefully, it is obvious that exercises like the Red Jelly Relaxation should only be entered into when it is safe and appropriate to close your eyes for a while. This is a very important safety rule, so I will repeat it: <u>only dip into the depths of your deeper mind and engage with your affirming statements, conditioning ideas and envisioning images when it is safe and appropriate for you to do so.</u> Seriously.

It's one thing to play yourself an affirmation programming subliminal recording while driving to work, but anything remotely hypnotic should only be utilized responsibly. Similarly, if you are not completely healthy in both mind and body, you are advised to get your doctor's approval before lowering your blood pressure or relaxing the grip you have over any suppressed cognitive content you might have lurking below consciousness.

The open mindset state of a true beginner's mind, is not an active engaged state of knowing. It's like disengaging from gear and drifting in neutral. Hopefully, it is clear to anyone that drives, that you cannot be in neutral and drive yourself. With a vehicle in neutral, you need a push from outside to move you. A truly neutral open state of mind, benefits greatly from being propelled forward by a trusted aid. For this reason, any purposeful thinking you do while relaxed, will tend to trigger beta wave activity. You want to feel pulled or drawn towards your goals and not have to push or force yourself.

Being a passive observer to an unfolding experience is still the best way to absorb uncritically. So, if you are going to take maximum advantage of the advice you've been confronted with in this chapter, you'd be well-advised to engage the services of someone you trust to influence you. Or at least make yourself a recording that you can close your eyes and relax to, while it does all the talking, leading you effortlessly into your deepest daydream state.

Now, I know that was a lot of information to absorb, but so that you do not have to reread this book too many times, let's take stock together and look at an overview of the important principles you've learned. My hope is that, like the nurses, you will find within these pages what specifically speaks to you and put it to good use. I sincerely hope that you will go beyond merely thinking that this stuff makes sense. I want you to utilize it far more than I care whether it makes intellectual sense to you or not. I didn't make any of it up, it all came from really clever people that I've learned a lot from. (Please refer to the Reference section if you would like to do some further reading on the subject.) Hopefully, you've learned a lot from me. Let's find out in our final chapter, after a quick overview of some key points from this one:

CHAPTER 9 SUMMARY

AKA:

WHAT YOU'VE LEARNED BY READING THIS CHAPTER

1. Trance states are a natural component to all learning that we've experienced.

2. Once learned, our opinions give us perspective to hold onto, that is easy to mistake as "the truth."

3. "Opening" your mind to ideas and other perceptions is possible if you feel safe to do so.

4. Physical relaxation is a feature of safety that is more conducive to an open mind than vigilance and tension.

5. Experiencing your Self-Propelling Sound-File™ in a profoundly relaxed state will tend to enhance the messages and make them more effective*.

---

*SAFETY WARNING: If you do develop a habit of trancing out while your sound file plays, DO NOT ever listen to it while driving ever again! I recommend making a separate sound file specifically designed to listen to while relaxing with your eyes closed.

DAVID FAIRWEATHER

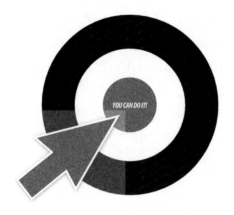

CHAPTER 10

MAKE IT HAPPEN

AKA

STOP WAITING AND TAKE ACTION

As we've seen, the human mind really is capable of some incredible things. It can keep us stuck if we believe it. It can move us without effort if we allow it. It can limit our awareness, allow us to explore limitless possibilities and even trick us into believing, that what we see is really there. You may have been tricked by your mind to believe that an obstacle in your way was insurmountable, or you may have been tricked into believing that you were happy with the way things are. You do not have to believe your own delusions, but you do have to put in some effort to overcome them, if you stand any chance of achieving more tomorrow than you believed was possible for you yesterday.

You cannot expect to experience a difference in your life or your career, if you always do what you've always done. To go beyond wishful thinking, you are going to need to do something about it. You need a plan to follow that has some chance of leading you where you want to go. Formulating and implementing a plan for success will take a little time to get straight in your head, and a little effort to gain momentum with. But once things get moving, it really will all get much easier.

Once you get off the launch pad, you will find that everything gets significantly easier, just like any rocket launch. For any skyward or spacebound mission, the vast majority of effort needs to be invested in the launch. After getting into orbit, there is no more fighting gravity and a lot less effort is required to get where you are headed. Most of your efforts are needed in the planning and propulsion stages. After that, it's almost effortless to keep going. Skimp on the preliminary stages or convince yourself that they are unnecessary, and you will probably find yourself struggling to stay motivated even if you start off that way. Getting motivated is one thing, but staying motivated is another. To get into the orbit of your goals, all your energy is needed in the launch stage. A good launch takes into account all the possible problems that could occur, and finds practical solutions for as many of them as possible, just in case.

LOCK ONTO THE RIGHT TARGET

There is a time to plan, and a time to act. If you've treated the planning stage seriously, everything else becomes a great deal more fun. Unguided missiles do not reliably or predictably hit targets that they are not locked onto. Even if you've made a tactical error in the planning stages, of course you can adjust your course as needed, so long as your programming is open to adjustments.

Back in my youth, when I worked for British Aerospace, a Ministry of Defence funded missile development company in England, one of the most terrible and amusing stories I was ever confronted with, involved a badly calibrated heat-seeking missile. Back then, missile tests were regularly conducted in remote areas of England and Wales, where the population was primarily grass and sheep. I assure you that it was not my fault, but one of the weapons of destruction that I was assigned to, decided for itself that the tank it had been targeted on, was not as invitingly warm as the nearby herd of sheep that it ultimately wiped out.

Now I love animals and I do not even eat mutton, or its baby equivalent, lamb, so I don't find the destruction of a bunch of innocent woolly mammals remotely funny. But there *is* something somewhat amusing about the incompetence of fallible aerospace engineers, prone to human error, in not considering the possibility that programming the missile to indiscriminately seek out heat might endanger clusters of warm-blooded creatures. There was an "Oh, crap!" moment before the carnage occurred, but by then, it was way too late to affect the course of the dumb bomb.

Thankfully, you are not a dumb destruction device. You definitely have the capacity to alter your course if needed. But without knowing which targets you are intending on hitting ahead of time, how would you know you'd made an error soon enough to avoid a potentially fatal collision? The average person puts very little effort into planning their life, and tends to spend more time planning their annual vacation than they do their career or their positive personal changes. The easiest way to stay stuck in the realm of the average person, is to do what average people do.

To boost yourself into the orbit of excellence, you'd be well-advised not to take on too much by aiming at multiple goals simultaneously. Airplanes only carry the fuel they need for the flight course plotted for them. Sure, they might have a little extra just in case they get rerouted or delayed from landing. But weighing them down makes them inefficient, as all the extra weight requires more effort for them to take off, and all the passengers would be required to pay the price, one way or another. So, avoid the temptation of taking on too much, and concentrate all your efforts on one immediate goal at a time. Otherwise you'll risk getting overwhelmed and feel your motivation getting diluted between multiple targets, each trying to get your undivided attention. You benefit from being focused, not scattered.

YOU HAVE TO START SOMEWHERE

Like someone keen to learn the piano or guitar, who deeply desires to be able to play every composition written by Beethoven or the Beatles, you are going to have to start by picking one song. When that eventually goes well, you can set your sights on another tune, and chances are, every subsequent song will become easier and easier to master faster and faster. Learning any artist's entire back catalogue would be like eating that metaphorical elephant. Pick a meal for now and don't worry about what is still left to digest.

Success builds upon success, and failure is far more encouraging of giving up. So, take the time needed to get really clear about your specific, smaller and achievable goals, that will take you at least one step along the pathway to reaching your big goal. Avoid focusing any energy on how far away you are from the mega success you've been dreaming about achieving. When it comes to your big juicy goal, set it and forget it as the maxim goes.

Keep in mind that the only way your mind is ever programmed, is via your five senses: smell, taste, feeling, sight and sound. In this book we've explored the three primary pathways for self-programming, those of auditory, visual and kinaesthetic. Of course, it's also possible to employ tasty treats and sweet smells as sensory self-rewards or associating them within full sensory envisioning. Even outside of envisioning, involving your olfactory and gustatory sense organs in your endeavours is a great idea (unless you are trying to slim down or get healthier).

Let's look at the top three that don't fail if you honestly put them to use. Anyone can get behaviour-changing information into their mind by teaching their brain what to do and when. Impressing motivating ideas into the deepest reaches of your mind, requires emotional responses to those ideas, in order to really glue them in. The more intense the emotion elicited by an idea, the less repetition is required to fix the idea in your mind. What really gets your attention, gets burned into your long-term memory as unforgettable.

The sights and sounds you experience make some impression on you, even if only subconsciously. The way they make you feel lets you know whether you like them or not. You might not know consciously why you like something. Once your subconscious has learned that you like something, like the colour blue; or the word blue; or the sound of the word blue; or the sight or the sound of the big blue ocean; or the way the water feels to float in or almost drown beneath, the response you have to the idea of "blue" becomes automatic.

With experience, your subconscious gets to understand how you perceive something. Its job then is to help you not need to think about it ever again, so you can use your precious brainpower and limited awareness to focus elsewhere and stay safe. We can lose sight of anything not in our immediate focus. That's a good thing if you don't want to be distracted. It's a good thing--unless you want to change your response to something, which is rare. But if you do want to change, don't worry, you can change on purpose. Changing your actions will change your feelings and changing your feelings will change your actions. Looking and listening aren't the same as seeing and hearing, but they'll each affect your feelings. Red lights and fire alarms motivate us into action if we are aware of them. Red lights and loud alarms that we cannot see or cannot hear, have no effect on us whatsoever.

What you see and what you hear affects how you feel. How you see things and what you tell yourself, determines what you do. If an undesirable response has already become hardwired and you want to override that previously programmed habit pattern, think logically only for a moment and use your senses for at least twenty-one to thirty consecutive days.

Let's take a brief look back at how you can use your senses going forward. Serious success requires getting serious about success, and you might need to work at making it into play. Science and any good parent will tell you that any form of play is the way to keep learning fun. The dopamine it triggers in an engaged brain makes focusing easy and continued engagement effortless. If you are serious about developing a better you, feel free to use my ACE acronym to help you cover all the main bases. Here is how to put it to work:

MAKING IT HAPPEN

HOW TO ACE YOUR GOALS™

Starting the moment that you are serious about achieving something, choose at least one element from each of the three ACE chapters on affirming, conditioning and envisioning, write down each of the commitments you are making, and decide to put them to work.

1. **A (Affirming)** – Get clear goals and actions and then commit them to memory. Tell yourself you can do it and hang around people that tell you, "You can do it!" If you've got a nagging voice of doubt in your mind, reassure yourself that you can do it and stop listening to doubt. If you really want something, don't listen to the voice of fear trying to hold you back from making a change. Unless your life would literally be placed in danger, it is probably only the voice of your ego scared of being forced to rethink itself into changing. Your brain can change, but it's not going to do so without some convincing.

2. **C (Conditioning)** – Set motivating rewards and deterrents and put them to use. Compel yourself to change and then at least pretend that you'll hold yourself accountable for your failures in some unpleasant way. Plan to succeed. Do not leave it to chance and your success won't be an accident. Better to stay away from self-defeating rewards like giving yourself a cigarette

because you've lasted an hour without having a cigarette. If you were trying to stop smoking, that would
just reinforce the idea that cigarettes are a pleasurable reward! If you struggle with responsibility and
accountability, employ the ego of an accountability
partner, therapist or coach, to compel you to stay on
track.

3.   **E (Envisioning)** – Go relax and see it happening in
your head. Imagine it as possible in your mind's eyes
and ears, and witness it happening in your imagination. Watch what successful people do, and see those
habits as possible for you.

The way you experience things in your mind determines
the experience you have of them. Make images in your
mind of fear and failure and you'll feel what it's like to
face them. Make images in your mind of succeeding and
the rewards of overcoming, and you'll feel far more motivated to make the changes necessary to make it happen.
Spend time picturing the way you want things to go, not
mentally rehearsing self-fulfilling failures.

You should record your goals and your progress along the way.
Knowing that you aren't as relaxed as possible when you are
thinking hard about anything, you might also need to consider
making a recording that you can put to use while you sit or lay
back and really, deeply relax.

LEARNING HABITS

If you strengthen neurological links by repeatedly connecting ideas and responses together, they will ultimately bind together and be bound to influence each other. The response will be unconscious and automatic by then, just like everything you aren't currently thinking of that you've learned up until now. Past learnings become automatic understandings, and understandings can be changed if you are open to changing them.

If you are prepared to look at things differently and tell yourself a different story, you might be surprised how different your life could really be. Really. The responses you learned some time ago can be changed. You can change old bad habits and build new healthy habits. Whether habit of thought, habit of behaviour, habitual ways of seeing things, or a habit of feeling a certain that way you'd rather not feel, you can change much more than you might imagine you can.

What you see for yourself and what you say about it will determine the experience you choose to have. Sure, you could surprise yourself, but this is a book about determination and drive, not accidents and exceptions. Put in the work, but allow the work to feel like play and make a game of it.

Now that you know what to do and why to do it, you have no excuses other than fear. Fear of change, fear of failure, fear of having your hopes dashed, or fear of how your life will change if you succeed. Some people fear who they'll become if they succeed in making a significant change. Whatever you do, do not pander to any kind of "success phobia." If you have even the slightest suspicion that you are in some way afraid of actually succeeding, please get help! If you try by yourself, your brain might try to convince you not to try changing it, but it *is* your brain when all is said and done. If you were afraid of trying, that would only be an emotional response to the way you perceive trying, and the meaning you are making of it, or have made of it in your mind.

Deep, deep at the back of your mind, if you have even the slightest feeling that you could succeed, I'd say, "Go for it, full out." Have faith that you'll figure out everything you don't yet know--if you remain focused. Use all of what you do know, (and so much more than that along the way), as you learn what it feels like being the you that thinks and feels successful and satisfied. Not tense and torn up, but relieved and reassured. Relaxed, self-assured and self-confident. Self-disciplined and rewarded accordingly.

All of that and more make up your subconscious-self that determines in reality what will or will not happen without your conscious choice. But by conscious choice, you can decide to exert an influence on your subconscious mind. You may or may not win, it depends on you. Succeeding with influencing an idea into your subconscious mind will just require a little determination. You can only get really determined to do something if you are emotionally compelled to do it.

COAX YOURSELF NOT TO QUIT

Compelling yourself with stimulating words and images will lead to subconscious success before success is expressed in reality. Sticking at it for a reasonable amount of time is going to be required. As long as you are reasonable about what is reasonable, then there is a reasonable chance that you'll succeed.

That's reasonable, isn't it? Like Ford thought, if you have a good mindset, that is what matters most. Mindset matters, don't forget that and act accordingly. Please.

You will accomplish whatever you keep focused on and never give up on (as long as it is possible). Is that clear? To help you get even clearer on your next step, let's take another quick look at what you've learned.

SUMMING IT ALL UP

AKA:

WHAT YOU'VE LEARNED BY READING THIS BOOK

1. Get clear on your goals.

2. Burn them into your brain.

3. Remain focused on them and accountable for taking the steps needed to achieve them.

Remember: **What you do determines how you feel, and how you feel determines what you do** – all influenced by the habitual ways you perceive things and what you tell yourself about them. Since your brain is always presenting a version of reality to you rather than an unedited, unbiased, raw reality, your "reality" is mostly a product of your own imagination. So use your imagination wisely. It's the intermediary between you and external reality. Want to change your reality? Change the way you think about it. The words and pictures you entertain in your mind is the place to start, regardless of what is happening outside of your head.

The number one thing you can do to get perpetual motivation started, is to get your goals onto a sound file and play it to yourself over and over and over again. It will take about fifteen to thirty minutes to make and you will never have to put any effort into listening to it. If you don't believe that it will influence you, try it for twenty-one days and you might just be surprised. What have you got to lose? Fifteen minutes? I think you can afford that, but what does the voice inside your head say?

Ok, so as a bare minimum, you'll be reminded on a daily basis what you'll do and why. With that done you'll be miles ahead of those with no goals or sketchy goals. Even without attempting to slow your mind down and absorb the messages in a trance, you will no longer be an unguided missile and you'll be answering questions about your goals like a top achiever or a high performer does: immediately and concisely.

Before we end our time together, you might like to check out those fifteen positive and fifteen negative words in a word search again to see what your RAS chooses to jump out at you now that you are fully pumped up and primed to take action? To save you from the trouble of searching for the word search puzzles, I've taken the trouble to put them all together into one big word search with all thirty words waiting for you to notice what you notice now.

WHICH WORD DO YOU SEE FIRST?

```
P P O S I T I V E X R I C H W G A M E X P Y K
L D P Q R S H I D E W F L I G H T B S T U C K
H E P V A M A Z I N G B C F O C U S C Q R E A
B S O Z I E N J O Y M Q O E B C B C O C E S Q
A T R E L A X A T I O N N C S S U S N S J T G
D R T U F A U F B Z T C T S T D R D F D E R R
J O U F I Q R E C O I L R D A T D T L T C A O
Z Y N L G B I A H I V I O T C R E S I S T T W
H C I O H P M R A E A E L L L P N O C Z V E A
O S T S T U P C C X T C Q D E X C I T I N G Q
P D Y E V R O S H F E S M P A N I C T T Z Y P
E S T R E S S D I V D I F F I C U L T D V H R
Y D R E F U S E E G H I F G W I N N E R R A A
Q T D X Q E I G V P B A N X I E T Y R H E T C
B P O S S I B L E X Q X Q R Y C X N R U P E T
N G H I F G L G Q P L A C E B O Z D I F L P I
E F F I C I E N C Y Y M A S Y N U O F R A E C
G D D A N G E R F F H A Q U H F F U I O C R A
A D D I C T I O N X X Z B L X I V B E Z E S L
T V B Z V T T Z V C R E A T E D Z T D E A I A
I Z S U C C E E D X H O P E L E S S J N B S Q
V M N O P L M L O V E Q R S A N M N O P L T A
E X C E L L E N C E Z D E M O T I V A T E D L
```

Well of course there is a lot more I could tell you and a great deal more I could try to teach you, but I promised I wouldn't go on and on and this isn't the last book I'm going to write. You could definitely find faster ways to get up to speed, the most obvious being to work with a coach or to go see a hypnotist. I'm not telling you to get help, I'm just saying that you should consider it if it would help?

For now, at least, it's time for you to put it to good use, if you are ok with that?

Great, now remember to read this again as there is a lot more than just the summary points weaved within these pages, often in the form of stories and asides. So, don't just rely on the summaries and check out **WINNING**-MINDSET.com if you need more help or you want to take advantage of the resources you'll find there – including the FREE AUDIO VERSION of this book!

As the community builds I'll be posting little extras there as well. You'll also get to see details of my seminars, training courses and executive coaching programs. I hope to meet you in person if we have not already had the pleasure. You are far greater than you yet believe.

GET IN TOUCH

I know you are going to gain a great deal of traction by implementing the methods covered between these pages and online, so it would be wonderful to hear from you about your successes. Share any specific techniques you found worked best for you. I encourage you to get in touch with me via the Winning Mindset website to share your stories, accolades and awards. I'll be offering rewarding ways that will make it fun to participate in the growing community of people who ACE their goals. Make sure you become one of them.

Now, MIND how you go and be GREAT.

And remember: YOU CAN DO IT!

YOU CAN

DO IT!

REFERENCES

AKA

ADDITIONAL RESOURCES YOU MAY ENJOY READING

- *Transforming Negative Self-Talk* – Steve Andreas

- *Tranceformations* – Dr John Grinder and Richard Bandler

- *Hypnotism, Imagination and Human Potentialities* – Dr. T.X. Barbar, Dr. Nicholas P. Spanos and John F. Chaves

- *How to Get From Passion to Success* – Richard Barker

- *Train Your Mind Change Your Brain* – Sharon Begley

- *Beyond the Relaxation Response* – Dr. Herbert Benson M.D

- *Your Maximum Mind* – Dr. Herbert Benson M.D

- *The Awakened Mind* – C. Maxwell Cade and Nona Coxhead

- *Keeping the Brain in Mind* – Shawn Carson and Melissa Tiers

- *Ultimate Motivation!* – Jason Christopher

- *Self Mastery Though Conscious Autosuggestion* – Dr. Émile Coué

- *The Seven Habits of Highly Effective People* – Dr. Stephen Covey

- *Flow* – Dr. Mihaly Csikszentmihalyi

- *Changing Belief Systems with NLP* – Robert Dilts

- *The Brain That Changes Itself* – Dr. Norman Doidge M.D.

- *The Science of Self-Hypnosis* – Adam Eason

- *Hypnotic Realities* – Dr. Milton H. Erickson M.D

- *Man's Search For Meaning* – Dr. Victor Frankl

- *Take Control of Your Subconscious Mind* – Anthony T. Galie

- *Human Givens. A New Approach to Emotional Health and Clear Thinking* – Joe Griffen and Ivan Tyrrell

- *I'm OK, You're OK* – Dr. Thomas Harris

- *Monsters and Magical Sticks. There's No Such Thing as Hypnosis* – Dr Steven Heller and Terry Steele

- *Planting the Seeds of Change* – Jack Hirsh

- *The Origin of Consciousness in the Breakdown of the Bicameral Mind* – Dr. Julian Jaynes

- *Autogenic Training* – Dr. Kai Kermani

- *How Expectancies Shape Experience* – Dr. Irving Kirsch

- *The Biology of Belief* – Dr. Bruce Lipton

- *Sleights of Mind* – Dr. Stephen Macknik and Susana Martinez-Conde with Sandra Blakeslee

- *Behaviour Modification* – Dr. Raymond G. Miltenberger

- *The Power of Your Subconscious Mind* – Dr. Joseph Murphy

- *Training Trances* – John Overdurf and Julie Silverthorn

- *Psychotherapy and Psychiatry* – Dr. Ivan P. Pavlov

- *Molecules of Emotion* – Dr. Candace Pert

- *Drive* – Daniel H. Pink

- *A User's Guide to the Brain* – Dr. John J. Ratey M.D

- *Stress Without Distress* – Dr. Hans Selye

- *Science and Human Behaviour* – Dr. B.F Skinner

- *Superlearning* – Sheila Ostrander and Lynn Schroeder with Nancy Ostrander.

- *You Are Not Your Brain* – Dr. Jeffrey M. Schwartz

- *The Clinical Effectiveness of Neurolinguistic Programming* – Lisa Wake, Richard M. Gray and Frank S. Bourke

- *The High-Performance Mind* – Anna Wise

- *:59 Seconds* – Dr Richard Wiseman

DAVID FAIRWEATHER

ABOUT YOUR AUTHOR

AKA

WHO IS DAVID FAIRWEATHER?

David's online stress and anxiety resources have been used by over half a million people worldwide. A Registered Psychotherapist and High-Performance Mindset Coach, David helps those serious about success adapt to the rapidly changing world of work and achieve the greatest level of excellence possible for them, despite life's obstacles.

Originally an Aerospace Design Engineer from England, David moved to Canada in the early 90's, teaching and consulting for some of the largest aerospace and automotive companies on the planet. He has always enjoyed a habit of breaking things down into their core components and then putting them back together as good as he found them or better.

At the turn of the millennium, he experienced a burnout by working an insane amount of overtime for too many weeks in a row without adequate breaks. It took time to accept that he wasn't superhuman and throw in the towel.

At the time it was the worst thing that could ever happen, as David's burnout lead to chronic fatigue and a musculoskeletal condition that came with carpal tunnel syndrome and ended his high-tech, computer dependent career.

David struggled initially to adapt, but eventually shifted his focus from the stress properties of aircraft and automobiles, to the stress capacity of human beings, the first being himself.

With a little help from some great people along the way and a few years of consistent effort, David successfully transitioned from teaching engineers how to program their design concepts into state-of-the-art, three-dimensional virtual reality software, to programming the mindsets of high-performers seeking to get to the next level in their actual reality without burning out. Having been exposed to numerous methods of meditation, self-hypnosis and mindfulness out of personal necessity, David forged a new path for himself by going back to school and pursuing a formal education in psychotherapy, stress management, coaching, psychology, philosophy, hypnosis and neurolinguistic programming (NLP).

While back in school, he became a college counsellor at Sutherland Chan and focused for a few years on helping pre-med level students determine and leverage their preferred learning styles (auditory, kinaesthetic or visual). Fascinated by the mental habits of high-performers, David went on to work as a researcher for York University's Faculty of Health, studying the impacts of stress and anxiety on performing at a high level under pressure in our high-tech world.

David facilitated workshops and lectured for their school of Nursing, and holds numerous instructor certifications in

Meditation, Self-Hypnosis and High-Performance Mind training / EEG Brainwave Biofeedback. It was during his time at York that David graduated from his psychotherapy program and was accepted by the College of Registered Psychotherapists of Ontario (aka CRPO) as a fully qualified Psychotherapist.

Today he lives in Toronto where he runs a successful solution-focused psychotherapy and results-focused coaching practice. In his spare time, he can be found breaking the law in his local ravine by walking his adorable but dumb dog Lulu off-leash, or talking to the squirrels, birds, rabbits and chipmunks that fill up daily on the seeds he spreads for them on his suburban patio. He has learned the hard way how to balance work and life and couldn't be happier with the results of working smart, not hard anymore.

He enjoys binging on politically incorrect British comedies on Netflix whilst trying to convince his entitled Persian cat Sherlock not to drink from his teacup. When he is not being provoked into teaching driver etiquette to Canadian drivers that clearly never studied the highway code (you know who you are), David can sometimes be found on the streets of Toronto surprising strangers that pass by with the impromptu hypnosis demonstrations that he films and publishes on his YouTube channel: **David Fairweather – YouTube**

He is currently focused on making a big difference in the results of business professionals and high achievers via his motivational speaking engagements, self-programming seminars and executive coaching programs. Every great leap forward begins not just by necessity, but by having the right target, and more importantly, the right mindset to do what needs to be done.

With the right mindset – you can do almost anything!!

Get in touch with David today if you want to get clear about your goals, develop great habits on purpose, or to make a shift in the mindset of your team.

WINNING-MINDSET.com

David@DavidFairweather.ca

Printed in Great Britain
by Amazon

19835331R00139